40 Days to Power Living®

Think, Eat & Live on Purpose

Featuring an Accelerated Coaching Program with

Harvard-Trained Business & Lifestyle Expert

Teresa Kay-Aba Kennedy

40 DAYS TO POWER LIVING® by Teresa Kay-Aba Kennedy
Published by Power Living Enterprises, Inc.
71 West 128th Street, Suite 3B
New York, NY 10027-3102
www.power-living.com

ISBN 978-1-59916-201-0

PRINTED IN THE UNITED STATES OF AMERICA

ACKNOWLEDGMENTS

This project is literally a gift from God, and owes a great deal to my parents – Janie Sykes-Kennedy and Dr. James Scott Kennedy. Both of them have been my gurus, my life teachers. When I was four years old, my Mom started introducing me to many of the spiritual and holistic health principles which form the basis of this book. My Dad, who passed away in 2005, speaks throughout this text as well. His Three Core Questions and emphasis on "specificity" guide our transformation process.

I must thank Mom, and my creative partner Richard L. Willard III – both trained as journalists, for editing this book at lightning speed; Evan Joseph for the cover photo; Gerald Robinson for cutting and styling my hair in preparation for the photo shoot; Alfred Fornay for doing my make-up for the shoot; and Chris Andreola for cleaning up the cover design. I am also grateful to my brother, James S. Kennedy, Jr. for being my creative and strategic partner from the beginning; my sister, Sheila Kennedy-Bryant for her constant support and encouragement; my brother-in-law, John Hope Bryant for his example of excellence; and my nephew, Daniel for his purposeful presence and for letting me use his essay, "Just Me and That's All."

I also thank my cousin, Leon Isaac Kennedy Jr., for being the strong elder of the Kennedy cousins; David Hinson for being my prayer partner and friend; and my long-time mentor, Jesse Hill Jr., as well as my cousin, Douglas Williams, Esq. for both being early supporters of my endeavors. All of these incredible people are my Circle of Support, and I love each of them dearly for always being there for me.

This is dedicated to your Highest Self.

TABLE OF CONTENTS

INTRODUCTION

Welcome to *40 Days to Power Living®*. I am SO excited to help you reshape your mind, body and spirit so that you can think, eat and live on Purpose!

Have you ever felt powerless? You can't seem to lose that extra 15 pounds. You're struggling with a health disorder. The deal you thought was "in-the-bag" just fell through. Your boss passed you over for a prime project. Your two-year-old has turned into a demon-child. Your funds have hit an all-time low. Your mate unilaterally decides to end the relationship. Any one of these scenarios might prompt you to cede your power – turn it over to the situation at hand. Power Living® is about taking control. It's about self-mastery. It is based on *charging* and *releasing* your energy along five key dimensions: spiritual, mental, physical, emotional, and environmental.

40 Days to Power Living® is a result of my time in the proverbial wilderness. I'd been a Type-A workaholic since I was 3 years old. As the story goes, I dropped out of nursery school because I wanted homework! This work ethic led to a very successful business career – receiving an MBA from the Harvard Business School and becoming one of the youngest Vice Presidents at MTV Networks. One day, though, I woke up and realized I had lost 20 pounds in a 2-week period. I was in the hospital for 10 days dying. They diagnosed me with Crohn's Disease – a severe digestive disorder. **I almost worked myself to death.** After nearly dying, I decided to start living. In learning how to heal myself, I learned about my Self and found my Purpose.

Now, my personal mission is to help people from ALL walks of life, live better lives. I operate the Ta Yoga House – one of the first yoga studios in Harlem, and Power Living Enterprises, Inc. – a multifaceted lifestyle company. My clients range from overworked executives (like I was!) to overscheduled stay-at-home moms. Certified in Holistic Health Counseling, Weight Management, Fitness and Yoga, I have also helped clients with a variety of ailments, ranging from Adult ADD, Asthma, Anorexia and Diabetes to Hypertension, Obesity, IBS and even Leukemia. The common thread for all of those coming to me is the desire to take control of their own lives, live more authentically, and achieve optimum energy and health - naturally.

What was my *thorn in the flesh* – an out-of-balance existence - is now my gift through the learning I share. I rebuilt my life from the ground up using spiritual and holistic health principles, and I can help you do the same.

"My grace is sufficient for you for my power is made perfect in weakness."
- 2 Corinthians 21:7

My story has been featured in media ranging from *The New York Times, Prevention, Yoga Journal,* and *O: The Oprah Magazine* to CNN, NBC's *Today in New York, Fox TV News,* and *The Hallmark Channel.* I am even in Oprah's book, *Live your Best Life!*, as well as featured in a German TV documentary. People around the world, who can't easily attend my workshops, have been asking me to share these principles. Well, here they are! **Please note that this book gives you *an accelerated version* of the Power Living® program; it is designed to help you jumpstart your transformation.** I usually teach clients these concepts over *at least* a three-month period. There will still be work to do after Day 40!

My Basic Truths

What we believe drives our lives. Let me share with you my guiding truths:

- No matter what your religious faith, no true transformation can happen without a spiritual foundation.
- The mind can be friend or foe – without mastery of it you will be a slave to it.
- The physical body is involved in everything. How you breathe, eat, drink, sleep and play affects your ability to fully experience your divine Purpose.
- Your heart must be involved in all action and communication in order to access your Source and navigate through the fire.
- Your environment affects your core energy – depleting or charging your power.

These truths represent the five dimensions of Power Living® - spiritual, mental, physical, emotional and environmental. *Power Living® is being spiritually connected, mentally focused, physically energized, emotionally engaged, and environmentally supported.* It is a way of being that allows life to *flow*. It is committing your energy to what you care about on a day-to-day basis.

On a practical level, Power Living® is knowing who you are and what you value and then organizing your life around it – what you do for work, who you choose to love, when and what you eat, how you communicate with your Self and others, etc. On a deeper spiritual level, it is living *on* Purpose, not just *with* purpose, allowing you to uncover and release your innate power.

What You Will Learn

We are a society addicted to quick fixes and radical solutions – from diets that eliminate entire food categories to invasive extreme makeovers. No *one* eating plan or form of exercise will work exactly the same for every body – that's one reason fad diets often fail. Crash dieting and simply changing on the outside will not address self-image issues and poor energy management skills.

You may want to lose weight, but is it just the pounds that have to go? You may want to change your job, but will that truly recast your outlook on life?

This Practice goes beyond just losing weight and obtaining a new work address. Over the next 40 days, I will give you the *framework* to craft your divinely appointed life… from the inside out. **It's a process of becoming conscious, moving you toward self-awareness and self-control.** It allows you to most effectively work in partnership with the Universe to live your best life possible. You will systematically learn how to implement the Five Principles of Power Living®:

1. **Live on Purpose** – You will delve deeper into your own values and beliefs, and align your spiritual energy to be fully Present and on Purpose.
2. **Tune your Mind to the Positive** – You will check your thoughts and language, and learn how to focus your mental energy to create positive manifestations and spur inspiration.
3. **Honor your Body** – You will learn the PWR® Foods, and "The 7 Rules of PWR® Eating," as well as how to exercise, breathe and sleep to maximize your physical energy for peak performance and optimum health.
4. **Be a Humble Warrior** – You will practice leading with your heart, and learn how to engage your emotional energy to cultivate an attitude of gratitude and build intimate connections, steady joy and strong faith in your path.
5. **Sanctify your Surroundings** – You will practice simplicity and specificity, and learn how to detoxify your environmental energy to sustain your flow and support your vision.

The first week is an overview, where you will use all of the principles in small ways. Then, each week we'll delve deeper into one principle. Also, at the beginning of each week, you'll receive a set of "PWR® Moves" – action steps representing the primary habits. Each step builds on the next. At the end of the 40 days, you will have a solid foundation for Power Living®! The Practice is laid out in a very doable, easy-to-use format. Every day, there are generally two pages to read and a couple of "Reality Check" self-assessment questions to answer. Use a separate journal to write out your answers if you like. Some people like to read through the whole book at once and then go back to do the exercises; others follow it day-by-day. Do what works for you. My goal is to give you the tools to make smart choices so you can make real changes. For 40 days, devote 15 minutes of your day to this Practice, and you will be rewarded over a lifetime. Note that we are working with a six-day week, so that you may rest and reflect on the seventh day. Over time, you will see that even on your day of rest, your outlook and behavior will be more positive.

The Power of 40 Days

You may be thinking, "Well, it's going to take more than 40 days to get *my* life together!" Actually, you're right. Transformation takes time. It took me seven years to reconstruct my life and I'm still evolving. It's a step-by-step unfolding. If you try to skip over some critical stages, you may find that you prolong your season in the wilderness. Part of the process is learning that it IS a process!

When making lifestyle changes, I've found that it generally takes *at least* six weeks, approximately 40 days, to really *begin* to feel the effect of natural mind-body-spirit techniques. You need to give your Core time to heal and come out of its shell.

You may actually want to rebel halfway through and go back to your old ways of thinking and acting. Start from where you are and stick with it! Our step-by-step approach may take a little longer than some of the "quick-fix" schemes on the market, but it will lay the groundwork for a lifetime of healthy and purposeful living.

"Anyone who is among the living has hope - even a live dog is better than a dead lion."
- Ecclesiastes 9:14

In the Bible, 40 days is often used as the ideal timeframe for renewal and transformation. We see this in the lives of Noah (Genesis 7:4), Moses (Exodus 24:18), Elijah (1 Kings 19:8), Ezekiel (Ezekiel 4:6), Jonah (Jonah 3:4) and Jesus (Matthew 4:2, Acts 1:3). It is also scientifically known that it takes approximately this same amount of time to form a habit. A neurotransmitter called dopamine acts on the brain's decision-making mechanisms to turn repeated patterns into habits.

As Aristotle said, "We are what we repeatedly do. Excellence then, is not an act, but a habit." Most people have habits they are not even aware of, from picking up a donut on the way to work, to negative self-talk. Bad habits can undermine progress for even high-potential people. Good habits can propel you to success.

Since the best way to overcome a habit is to replace it with another one, our strategy is to *add* positive behaviors and simply make you aware of potentially harmful habits. This Practice is not about deprivation, it's about observation and moderation.

Purpose With Results™

The ultimate goal of *40 Days to Power Living®* is for you to get in the habit of consciousness and action, allowing you to realize true **PWR® - Purpose With Results™**.

I believe that we are moving toward a New World... a world where POWER is not defined by how much control you have over *others*, but how much control you have over your *Self*. It's not about how many things you *acquire*. It's about how many people you *inspire*.

> "You would have no power over me if it were not given to you from above."
> - John 19:11

The Old World valued *conformity*. This New World values *uniqueness*. In this New World, you drop the "O" (approval from *others*), and drop the "E" (attachment to *external* things), and realize true PWR® - Purpose With Results™!

We're talking about Purpose with a big "P" – that overarching vision that drives your life that allows the essence of YOU to shine through; Thought and Action resulting in a Positive Willful Reaction.

This PWR® is:

- available to all,
- unique in each of us,
- allows you to project an energy that attracts, and
- comes with a Lifetime Guarantee.

Your ultimate goal is to activate this PWR®. The only requirements are that it comes from *within*, and it must be charged and released *every day*.

I challenge you to Commit to Life *right now*. It's time to move from the *intellectual realm* (knowing what to do) to the *experiential realm* (actually doing it). Don't wait. Life is in THIS moment. If you are willing to open your eyes, I will lead you on a journey to find your Self! I will lead you to Power Living®!

Are you ready? If so, I encourage you to sign the contract on the next page symbolizing your commitment to becoming an active participant in your life in order to live the most *purposeful and powerful* life possible!

COMMIT TO LIFE CONTRACT

==========================

Today, I Commit to LIFE! I commit to actively seek and further my Life Purpose on a daily basis. I understand that I have the Power of Choice, my choices in the past created my experiences of today, and my choices today are creating my experiences of tomorrow. I now choose to define my own success and design my own life. I am ready to make values-driven decisions and be Present each moment along my journey. I commit to living a conscious life. I am ready to start Power Living® TODAY!

____

Today's Date

____

Name

Teresa Kay-Aba Kennedy __________________

Your Power Living® Coach

The Power Living® Practice

Every week you'll receive a set of **"PWR® Moves"** – action steps that reflect the Five Principles of Power Living® which can lead you to true PWR® - Purpose With Results™. They are represented by the 5 trigger words below: Reflect, Focus, Re-Fuel, Connect and Release. Over the next 40 days, you'll learn more about each area picking up specific strategies to enhance your life spiritually, mentally, physically, emotionally and environmentally.

Week 1:

Overview

<u>Week 1 – PWR® Moves</u>

So, here we go! Our first week, we'll ease into the primary habits. A critical aspect of the Practice is self-awareness, so start a Daily Lifestyle Log on page 27. We'll only do this for 6 days, so try to stick with it. Note all activities – work, eating, if you smoke, etc. Also, track your overall progress for the items below on page 19.

1. **REFLECT.** Develop a Reflective Ritual. We'll start with only *10 minutes a day* – 5 minutes in the morning to ponder the Three Core Questions on page 21 and review your intentions for the day, and 5 minutes in the evening to reflect on what you accomplished and plan for the next day.

2. **FOCUS.** Tune your mind with positive affirmations. Use the example below to start. Read it quietly and then aloud. Repeat it at morning, lunch, before bed, and anytime your mind needs tuning. Constant repetition out loud is important.

   "I am priceless. My worth does not depend on my title, money, appearance or what other people think. As a spiritual being with a divine mission, I am intrinsically priceless."

3. **RE-FUEL.** Two elements are exercise and hydration.

   a. **Sweat.** Move for at least *10 minutes a day,* for the 6 days of our week. We'll be increasing the time period progressively. Right now, just break a sweat. If you don't already have a routine, walking is a good place to start.
   b. **Hydrate.** Drink at least 8 glasses of purified water a day.

4. **CONNECT.** Every day determine ways to experience joy in the little things – a child's hug, sunshine, another day alive!

5. **RELEASE.** Let go of *one* bind every day- a thought, a thing, a commitment, a person, a debt; anything holding you back.

Give it your best. Log your Progress.

Week 1 – Progress Log

As you receive PWR® Moves each week, rate yourself daily in each area using a 1 – 5 scale (1 =not successful, 5 =very successful).

Action	Day1	Day2	Day3	Day4	Day5	Day6
REFLECT						
Reflect 10 min.						
FOCUS						
Affirmations						
RE-FUEL						
Sweat 10 min.						
Hydrate 8 glasses						
CONNECT						
Experience Joy						
RELEASE						
Release 1 Bind						

Accomplishments/Challenges/Notes to Self:

Day 1

Take Stock

"Take the first step in faith.
You don't have to see the whole staircase, take the first step."
- Dr. Martin Luther King, Jr.

Congratulations for choosing to follow The Power Living® Practice! Sometimes we can get so busy with the mundane aspects of living we forget to dedicate sacred time to do the real work of life. You've just taken the first step.

In order to initiate change, you must acknowledge where you are. Though truthfulness is empowering, it is not easy to face - which is why we often avoid it. It's bad enough to tell a lie to another, but to deceive your Self is just plain foolish... yet we do it anyway!

> "The truth will set you free. But first, it will piss you off."
> - Gloria Steinem

- "One more (drink, donut, etc.) won't make a difference."
- "He really does love me (even though he never calls)."
- "I *need* this (pair of shoes, new car, etc.)."
- "That didn't hurt me (even though I am crying inside)."

Over the next 40 days, I will require just one thing of you: **actively search for *your* truth, living with your eyes wide open.** If you do this, you will be well on your way to Power Living®!

Two Foundation Concepts

My Dad, Dr. James Scott Kennedy, was a professor, philosopher, playwright and preacher. He would often talk about "**specificity**" - *being specific about your thoughts, words and actions* - and then ask his children to ponder his **Three Core Questions**:

- **Who Am I?**
- **Where Am I?**
- **What Must I Do To Be Me?**

It took me almost dying to finally understand the depth of those very specific words - questions which form the basis of The Power Living® Practice. I now understand them to mean: Who am I at my Core? Where am I along my path? What MUST I do *every day* to be authentically me? Not what *should* I do... or what *could* I do... what *MUST* I do! In using these three questions, I help clients envision their Core Self, take an honest look at where they are currently, and then create very specific habits to close the gap.

When my Dad passed away in 2005, I realized that by honoring these Three Core Questions every day and by being very specific in his choices, he led a full life... in fact he *truly lived all the days of his life.*

"For when David had served God's purpose in his own generation, he fell asleep."
- Acts 13:36

- Looking back, will you be able to say that you've lived ALL the days of your life?
- Are you living every day *full in* or *spread thin*?
- Are you living your divine destiny? Do you even know what it is?
- Do you have the physical energy to achieve your vision?
- If this were your last day, would you have fulfilled your Purpose in this lifetime?

The Process of Letting Go

The entire Power Living® Practice is based on *letting go of the unnecessary things so that you can let the sacred in.* The concept of letting go applies most tangibly to *things,* such as the "skinny jeans" you still have from high school or the dusty fax machine that doesn't work anymore. When you finally clear the physical clutter from your world, you can visibly *see* the space it creates.

> "To be wronged is nothing unless you continue to remember it."
> - Confucius

What is harder to deal with is *recognizing and releasing emotional strongholds,* such as the responsibility for your son who has a drug addiction or the dreams of what might have been if you had followed your heart. Holding on to unproductive emotions - such as guilt, shame, fear and anger - is fertile ground for even more dysfunctional feelings to grow, such as regret, pain, obsessive thinking, and bitterness. Living in denial and not owning the consequences of your actions, leads you down the path of self-destruction. Similarly, trying to "save" another person by constantly "fixing" a situation leads them down the rocky road of dependency and decreased self-esteem, which leads to a host of other problems. Holding on simply holds you where you are, and prevents you, and possibly, another person, from growing.

Letting go is the first step in the journey toward a more authentic life. When you let go emotionally, you're not throwing things away, you are simply leaving things as they are without attachment to them. You are liberating your Self and others from suffering. Think of things, relationships, and life itself, as precious gifts that are on loan to you. Cherish the moments, learn from the experiences, and move on. Let go of the assumption that you know what is right. Have faith in the Universe and trust that no matter what happens ALL is working for your Highest Good. Instead of simply surviving, make a commitment to thrive.

Reality Check

To start the Practice, today you're going to do an overall check of where you are right now. Then, over the next five days, you will look at each principle and get some of the primary habits started. Right now, from your current perspective, answer the following:

Who Am I?

Who am I at my Core? Who am I becoming? Describe your Authentic Self. Who are you at your best? Think about the layers of who you are - such as wife/husband, mother/father, daughter/son, woman/man, friend, executive, student, caregiver - and then strip away these labels and look at what else you find. For example, "I am creative." "I am a healer." "I am generous."

____

____

____

____

____

____

____

____

Remember to sweat for at least 10 minutes today.

Where Am I?

Where am I along my path? How big is the gap between where you are now and who you are meant to be? Take a moment to think about where you are right now:

- **Spiritual**: Do I take time to cultivate my inner life? Am I living my core values? Do I operate by faith or by fear?
- **Mental**: Do my thoughts support my vision? Am I focused, engaged and productive at work?
- **Physical**: Am I honoring my body by how I breathe, eat, drink, sleep, and exercise?
- **Emotional**: Am I able to make deep connections? Do I experience joy every day? Do I have the patience to succeed?
- **Environmental**: Does my environment - space, people, things - support my life vision? Are my finances reflecting a flow in my life or blockage?

5					
4					
3					
2					
1					
	Spiritual	**Mental**	**Physical**	**Emotional**	**Environmental**

An electrocardiogram, or EKG, records the electrical activity of the heart over time. View this as your "PWR® EKG" – charting your energy utilization to help you see how close you are to achieving true PWR® - Purpose With Results™. Decide what number represents your current state in each category: 1 = disappointing, 5 = ideal. Then, for each category, mark a large dot on the line corresponding to that number. Connect the dots to see if your energy is being optimally utilized or if it is off-balance. If you "flat-line" on 1 across the board, then we have a lot of work to do!

What Must I Do To Be Me?

What *must* I do every day to be authentically me? Look at the results of your energy utilization. Where are you in relation to where you want to be? How does your life need to change in order to live more authentically? Be honest, realistic and very specific. Start where you are. We will revisit this over time.

What do I need to add to my life?

1. ____

2. ____

3. ____

4. ____

5. ____

What do I need to remove?

1. ____

2. ____

3. ____

4. ____

5. ____

Make sure your goals are SMART –
Specific, Measurable, Attainable, Realistic, and Time-specific.

What would I like to accomplish over the next 40 days?

How would a successful outcome make me feel?

Daily Lifestyle Log

Date: ____________

Time	Activity	Mood	Efficiency

Note: When eating, log the item you ate, estimated calories if possible, your mood before and how you feel 1 hour later.

Principle #1: Live on Purpose

"Many are the plans in a man's heart,
but it is the Lord's purpose that prevails."
-- Proverbs 19:21

Live on Purpose, the first principle of Power Living®, is about aligning your spiritual energy to be fully Present and on Purpose.

No matter what a person comes to me for – to lose weight, manage stress, change careers, build self-esteem - our work always starts at the Core: *Are you living a purposeful and authentic life?* Once we address this issue, undoubtedly the other pieces fall more easily into place.

Purpose with a big "P"

Have you ever fallen in love? Do you remember the feeling? You couldn't wait to see your sweetheart. Just the thought of your love brought a smile to your face. You would steal moments together. People would say, "You're glowing. You must be in love."

How would you like to fall in love with life? Your heart is racing as you wake up in the morning with excitement about the new day. You capture moments along the way. Life is good. People will say, "You're glowing." Living on Purpose is like falling in love. Life *flows.*

For many years, I was working *with* purpose, but not living *on* Purpose. I went from one unconnected goal to the next – negotiate another deal, get a bigger home, obtain the grand promotion, etc. I achieved just about everything I set my mind to do. Although it was very satisfying from an ego-standpoint, there was still something bothering me. I felt like I was drifting through life. From the outside, it looked like I had a clear direction. From the inside, I was lost. Yet, I didn't really notice the discrepancies in my own life until it was almost too late.

Now I know what was causing the discomfort. When you live *outside of your Purpose,* you exist in a state of perpetual frustration and stress. Satisfaction is fleeting. You can have material wealth, yet be spiritually poor. On the other hand, when you are *living on Purpose,* you feel a sense of peace, experience progress, and release your divine, spirit-based power. You come from a place of joy, passion and self-less service. You can achieve true prosperity, on your own terms.

Purpose as an Energy Source

If your primary goal is to lose weight, you may be thinking, "Why should I be focusing on Purpose? That's such a heavy topic… I just want to shed some pounds!"

Your Purpose is your reason for being and is a major energy source. Out of 6 billion people on this Earth, there is only one YOU – with your special combination of thoughts, talents, look, personality, and quirks. You are a crucial piece in this Universal puzzle.

> "Knowing others is wisdom, knowing yourself is enlightenment."
> - Lao-tzu

Your greatest work is to discover why you're here, and then nurture and share that gift.

When you get a glimpse of your Purpose, it becomes uncomfortable to simply exist. Your Purpose becomes a strong personal motivator - it wakes you up in the morning and fuels your action. It's related to everything you do in life and *how* you do it. If you view your entire life as an offering to the Universe, every thought, word and action becomes sacred.

Seek Revelation

Your Purpose is revealed. It is not something you conjure up, and you typically don't just stumble upon it. Understanding your Purpose generally requires you to be an active investigator and student. It will be revealed to you at the right time, given that you are ready to receive. You must do the work of discovery. You must remove the blocks so you can achieve clarity.

We often give more thought to what we will do with our vacation days, than what we will do with our lives. We will take time to watch a TV show, but not take a moment to know the subtleties of our own story.

> "You will seek me and find me when you seek me with all your heart."
> - Jeremiah 29:13

The process of reflection provides a source of power. It allows you to look back and make sense of what happened, and look forward to prepare for the future. How often do you take the time to reflect on your decisions and actions? How much time do you spend *actively* seeking your Purpose? How serious are you about living a powerful life?

Regardless of your religion, it is important to become inward-focused and cultivate a ritual that includes some form of daily contemplation. Contemplation is the act of thoughtful observation or study. It is a form of mantra mediation that is focused on spiritual matters, and can be coupled with prayer. It is not tied to any form of religion. It simply allows you to tap into the voice within to be open for inspiration and direction.

Reality Check

Every day we'll pause to do a "Reality Check." Today we're going to get started aligning your **spiritual energy**. From your current perspective, answer the following:

When do I REFLECT? Think about the "Where Am I?" exercise on page 24. How did utilization of your spiritual energy rate?

How many minutes a day do I spend in reflection? ________

What am I currently doing to charge my spiritual energy and find clarity of vision? (e.g. quiet time, reading, prayer, etc.)

____

____

____

____

How can I manage it better?

____

____

____

____

Remember to fill out your daily lifestyle log today.

Daily Lifestyle Log

Date: ____________

Time	Activity	Mood	Efficiency

Note: When eating, log the item you ate, estimated calories if possible, your mood before and how you feel 1 hour later.

Principle #2: Tune your Mind to the Positive

"For as he thinketh in his heart, so is he."
-- Proverbs 23:7

Tune your Mind to the Positive, the second principle of Power Living®, is about tuning your mental energy to create positive manifestations, achieve focus, and spur inspiration.

After encouraging a client to reflect on the Three Core Questions, the next thing I normally check is the *mental frequency*. Is her language negative and self-effacing, or positive and affirming? This will affect the outcome of any goal she is trying to achieve – whether it's getting fit or changing careers.

> "As the mind, so the man; bondage or liberation are in your own mind."
> - Sanskrit saying

The Tape in the Head

We all have that tape in the head - the inner enemy - constantly throwing bombs on our best dreams:

- "Why will they listen to me?"
- "I need more skills, money, looks…"
- "I could *never* get that done…"

According to most ancient philosophies, if you have controlled your mind, you have controlled everything. Thoughts – the movement of consciousness - have power and take form. There is a direct Mind-Matter connection. Each thought has a corresponding physiological effect. Science has shown us, for example, that a mind filled with thoughts of fear can cause acceleration of the heart rate.

Your attitude – about your Self, others and life itself – affects everything you do. It can result in high or low self-esteem. It can draw people to you, or repel them. It can make a situation joyous or simply bearable. In fact, the quality of your thoughts and your disposition is often more important than mental capacity in terms of predicting long-term success.

"Your thoughts are your spiritual capital. Invest them well and your subconcious will take over and react beautifully, expressing itself in your world."
- Dr. Stuart Grayson

Affirmations -- simple statements you repeat to your Self -- are a powerful tool for developing a positive frame of mind so you can achieve your life vision. The power of affirmation is based on the belief that thought or consciousness is a dynamic field of energy which projects and draws into your life exactly what you demand of it. Some call it the Law of Cause and Effect.

Use your mind for good – to heal your Self, to create wealth, to share joy, to direct your life and achieve your individual destiny. Be conscious of your internal chatter, as well as your vocabulary. Each day, try to find at least *one* positive thing in your life. Any day that starts with an uplifting outlook will be less stressful and much more productive. And, remember, merely to abstain from negative thinking is not enough, there must be *active right thinking* to create positive manifestations.

Reality Check

Today we're going to get started tuning your **mental energy**. From your current perspective, answer the following:

When and on what do I FOCUS? Think about the "Where Am I?" exercise on page 24. How did utilization of your mental energy rate?

How many minutes a day do I spend absolutely focused? ______

What am I currently doing to charge my mental energy and achieve/maintain focus on my vision? (e.g. affirmations, meditation, scheduled work breaks, etc.)

____

____

____

____

How can I manage it better?

____

____

____

____

Remember to drink at least 8 glasses of purified water today.

Daily Lifestyle Log

Date: ______________

Time	Activity	Mood	Efficiency

Note: When eating, log the item you ate, estimated calories if possible, your mood before and how you feel 1 hour later.

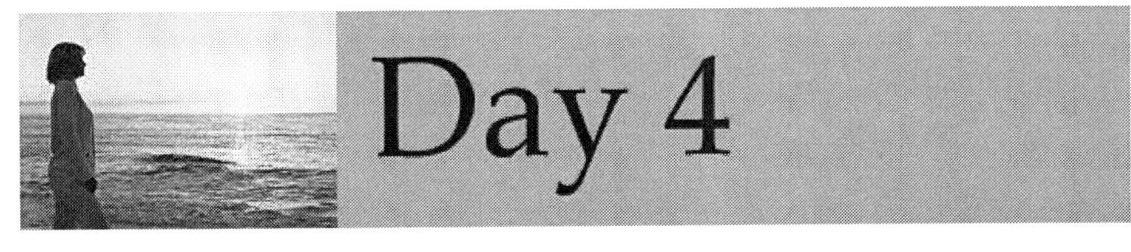

Principle #3: Honor your Body

"The first wealth is health."
- Ralph Waldo Emerson

Honor your Body, the third principle of Power Living®, is about maximizing your physical energy for peak performance and optimum health.

My office is on the third floor of a brownstone. If a client comes up the stairs and is already winded by the time he gets to me, I know we have some work to do!

Think about your own energy:

- Do I wake up refreshed and energetic, without using coffee or other sources of caffeine?
- Do I run out of steam at points during the day?
- Can I walk up a flight of stairs without being winded?
- Do I have the energy to fulfill my goals?

Most people spend more time and energy taking care of their cars, than their bodies. Instead of consuming premium fuel and paying attention to their "mileage," they fill up on sludge and drive themselves into the ground. As spiritual beings having a human experience, it is crucial for us to honor this temple that houses our souls.

Taking care of your Self – paying attention to how you eat, drink, exercise, sleep, and breathe -- is not a vain pursuit. **How you manage your lifestyle habits is a fundamental issue of Purpose.** It affects your ability to succeed in life, fueling you on your road to success. It is, in fact, *a necessity* in order to have *the energy* to achieve your PWR®. Otherwise you may just run out of gas along the way. If you ignore your body, you're simply being selfish – robbing your loved ones and others of your Core essence.

> "Take care of your body with steadfast fidelity. The soul must see through these eyes alone; if they are dim, the whole world is clouded."
> - Goethe

The Optimal Health Equation

Optimum health is about *balance* – a state where the body operates efficiently and the mind is alert so that the spirit may soar. If you treat your whole Self right, you will naturally come to your ideal weight, have full energy, and enable the body to heal itself. The first step toward optimal health is **self-awareness** – understanding your own patterns.

- When, how and what do I eat and drink?
- How much uninterrupted sleep do I get a night?
- How often do I sweat, stretch, and strengthen?
- How do I manage my energy throughout the day?

The next step is **self-control** – making smart choices. Although it is an individual journey, over the next few weeks I will give you some rules of the road. As you begin to Live on Purpose and have an over-arching vision for your life, the path toward self-awareness and self-control becomes smoother. It helps to have a motivating WHY to it all. Then, the HOW simply becomes about information and action.

Reality Check

Today we're focused on maximizing your **physical energy**. From your current perspective, answer the following:

How do I RE-FUEL? Think about the "Where Am I?" exercise on page 24. How did utilization of your physical energy rate?

How many minutes a day do I spend fully energized? ________

What am I currently doing to charge my physical energy so I am consistently fueled to achieve my goals? (e.g. balanced eating, adequate sleep, regular exercise, etc.)

____

____

____

____

How can I manage it better?

____

____

____

____

Remember to log your progress today.

Know your Numbers

Weight: ______ Height: _______ BMI: _______

Body mass index (BMI) is a measure of body fat based on height and weight that applies to both adult men and women. Find your number below:

Body Mass Index

Weight in Pounds

Height in Feet and Inches	120	130	140	150	160	170	180	190	200	210	220	230	240	250
4'6	29	31	34	36	39	41	43	46	48	51	53	56	58	60
4'8	27	29	31	34	36	38	40	43	45	47	49	52	54	56
4'10	25	27	29	31	34	36	38	40	42	44	46	48	50	52
5'0	23	25	27	29	31	33	35	37	39	41	43	45	47	49
5'2	22	24	26	27	29	31	33	35	37	38	40	42	44	46
5'4	21	22	24	26	28	29	31	33	35	37	38	40	41	43
5'6	19	21	23	24	26	28	29	31	33	34	36	37	39	40
5'8	18	20	21	23	24	26	27	29	31	32	34	35	37	38
5'10	17	19	20	22	23	24	26	27	29	30	32	33	35	36
6'0	16	18	19	20	22	23	24	26	27	29	30	31	33	34
6'2	15	17	18	19	21	22	23	24	26	27	28	30	31	32
6'4	15	16	17	18	20	21	22	23	24	26	27	28	29	30
6'6	14	15	16	17	19	20	21	22	23	24	25	27	28	29
6'8	13	14	15	17	18	19	20	21	22	23	24	25	26	28

Underweight Healthy Weight Overweight Obese

	Your Number:	Normal/Good Range:
Blood Pressure:	____________	*120/80 mmHg*
Blood Glucose:	____________	*4 to 8mmol/l*
Total Cholesterol:	____________	*Less than 200 mg/dL*
HDL: ("good" cholesterol)	____________	*60 mg/dL or above*
LDL: ("bad" cholesterol)	____________	*100-129 mg/dL*
Waist Measurement:	____________	*Women >35in. Men >40in.*

Notes: 1) Blood glucose is higher after meals and usually lowest in the morning. 2) To measure your waist, place a tape measure around your bare abdomen just above your hip bone. Be sure that the tape is snug, but does not compress your skin, and is parallel to the floor. 3) BMI does not show the difference between fat and muscle, so it does not always accurately predict when weight could lead to health problems – particularly for people who are very short (under 5 feet) or have a lot of muscle.

Know your History

It is important to know if you are predisposed to certain diseases.

What is my family health history? Are there certain illnesses that seem to run in your family? Find out and note them here.

How is/was the health of my father and mother?

How is/was the health of my siblings and other close relatives?

What is my chief health concern?

How can I change my habits *now* to reduce my risk of disease?

Daily Lifestyle Log

Date: ____________

Time	Activity	Mood	Efficiency

Note: When eating, log the item you ate, estimated calories if possible, your mood before and how you feel 1 hour later.

Principle #4:
Be a Humble Warrior

"To be a warrior is to learn
to be genuine in every moment of your life.
Success and failure are your journey."
- Chogyam Trungpa

Be a Humble Warrior, the fourth principle of Power Living®, is about engaging your emotional energy to cultivate an attitude of gratitude, and build intimate connections, steady joy, and strong faith in your path.

Do you ever feel like life is a battle? You're taking time to reflect every day, you're being a good steward of the talents you've been given... and things *still* seem hard? Remember when I said, "Transformation takes time?" There's a reason for that! Ask yourself:

- How do I respond when things don't happen the way I want them to?
- If there was a chance I could fail at something I really wanted to do, would I do it anyway?
- If my success were *guaranteed*, would I have the courage and patience to follow the road less traveled?
- Am I happy when someone else achieves, or am I secretly envious?

Learning how to be a humble warrior allows you to take success and failure with an equally peaceful heart. According to ancient text, the key to warriorship is not being afraid of who you are. It is based on cultivating a combination of fearlessness, egolessness, goodness, discriminating awareness, and a willingness to change.

Society has conditioned us to avoid pain. Therefore, many of us fear change and become paralyzed, not realizing that being stuck in one state of being kills the soul and stunts our growth. The only way to build a truly successful life is to push past your comfort zone and allow your character to be refined.

> "We either make ourselves miserable or we make ourselves strong. The amount of work is the same."
> - Carlos Castaneda

Ironically, as we avoid pain, we are often blocking joy. We may pursue material things which we believe will make us happy, but they are only temporary band-aids. The wound of not following your heart goes much deeper when it becomes regret and resentment. Our vision becomes cloudy, leading us to ignore the simple things that can stir the soul. Developing a sense of your own intrinsic value and gratitude for all of the good that is already present in your life is the foundation for becoming a true warrior.

Face Fear with Faith & Action

As I mentioned above, one aspect of being a humble warrior is fearlessness. Countless people fall short of their divine destinies because of a simple four-letter word: FEAR. From mild anxiety to panic attacks and phobias, fear can immobilize decision making, stifle your motivation, lock you in self-destructive behavior, and be a roadblock to growth.

Fear has power. It is an important emotion that alerts you to perceived danger, and can be a useful motivating tool. The problem occurs when the danger is not real: **F**alse **E**vidence **A**ppearing **R**eal. When fear creeps in, turn it around:

- **F**ocus on your Desired Result
- **E**xplore your Resistance
- **A**ssess your Options
- **R**espond by Taking Action

When you face fear, it shrinks; but if you refuse to face it, it grows. The greatest weapons against fear are faith and action. Over the next few weeks, I'm going to encourage you to face your fears so you can create a new reality.

> "For God has not given us the spirit of fear; but of power and love, and of wisdom."
> - 2 Timothy 1:7

We'll learn techniques to embrace change, count it all joy, lead with love, listen to connect, nurture your Self, and pause & play. As you will discover, **the surest path to success is through the fire**. Making this journey depends on the strength of your Core and the faith in your path.

Reality Check

Today we're focused on engaging your **emotional energy**. From your current perspective, answer the following:

How do I CONNECT? Think about the "Where Am I?" exercise on page 24. How did utilization of your emotional energy rate?

How many minutes a day do I spend truly connecting with my Self and others? __________

What am I currently doing to charge my emotional energy so that I keep the faith in my vision and feel peace along the way? (e.g. playtime, relationship time, pure laughter, self-care, etc.)

____

____

____

____

How can I manage it better?

____

____

____

____

Remember to seek joy today.

Daily Lifestyle Log

Date: ____________

Time	Activity	Mood	Efficiency

Note: When eating, log the item you ate, estimated calories if possible, your mood before and how you feel 1 hour later.

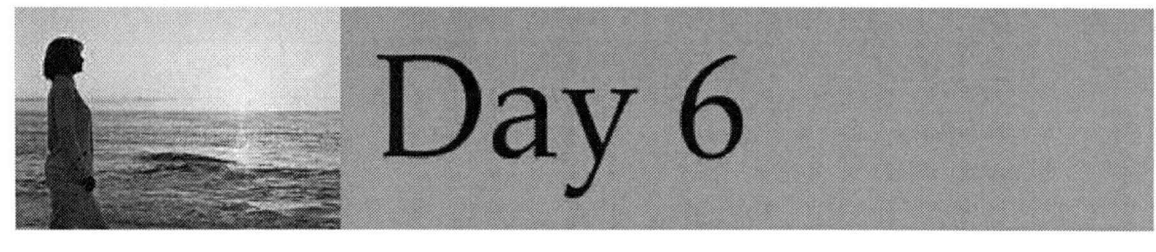

Principle #5: Sanctify your Surroundings

"The ability to simplify means eliminate the unnecessary so that the necessary may speak."
- Hans Hofmann

Sanctify your Surroundings, the fifth principle of Power Living®, is about detoxifying your environmental energy to sustain your flow and support your vision. This means *everything* around you, including all of the choices regarding your external life. Think about the following:

- Do I feel at home in my house?
- Is my office cluttered with unnecessary things?
- Am I hoarding money or giving power to debt?
- Do the people around me charge or drain my energy?

Simplicity is not about deprivation or income level. It's about living deliberately and making specific choices. One of the greatest gifts given to us by our Creator is the ability to make choices. You have the right to choose what you wish to experience. If you choose destructive behavior, you are likely to experience suffering. If you choose loving behavior, you are likely to experience joy. The same power goes into creating your environment. **To live more simply is to live thoughtfully in the Present and to organize your life around your Purpose.**

The Elements of Flow

Life is about flow; some things you simply have to let go! Life is based on circulation. Every sixty seconds your blood circulates in the body. If some area of the blood's passageway is obstructed, the blood becomes congested and its life-sustaining flow is interrupted.

The same principle is expressed in how we manage our energy and possessions. Do you mindlessly acquire things? Do you think *more* is better? Do you have a scarcity mentality? What are you holding on to that is holding you back? Are you actively supporting your flow?

Streamline your life. It's hard to think clearly when you are surrounded by clutter, toxic people or debt. Less can mean more. Every day you must let go. Clear away the excess – thoughts, things, bills, commitments, and relationships. Create order internally and externally. Make time and space for the things you love – get rid of the rest.

> "Simplicity, clarity, singleness: these are the attributes that give our lives power and vividness and joy."
> - Richard Halloway

Over the next few weeks, we will learn techniques to Sanctify your Surroundings: define the essentials, clear and cleanse, satisfy the senses, let the outside in, distance the doubters, and seek financial serenity. As you clear away the excess and things that do not support your success, you make room for abundance. If you accept the concept of flow, you also become more open to giving freely. You know that it will come back to you, and you'll know when enough is enough.

Reality Check

Today we're focused on detoxifying your **environmental energy**. From your current perspective, answer the following:

How do I RELEASE? Think about the "Where Am I?" exercise on page 24. How did utilization of your environmental energy rate?

How many minutes a day do I spend detoxifying my environment? ________

What am I currently doing to charge my environmental energy to support my flow? (e.g. clearing clutter, distancing toxic people, reducing debt, etc.)

____

____

____

____

How can I manage it better?

____

____

____

____

Remember to release one bind today.

Daily Lifestyle Log

Date: ____________

Time	Activity	Mood	Efficiency

Note: When eating, log the item you ate, estimated calories if possible, your mood before and how you feel 1 hour later.

A PWR® Moment

Just Me and That's All

The Power of Authenticity

In second grade, my nephew was asked to write an essay about someone he would like to be like. As his friends wrote about celebrities and well-known people, this is what Daniel wrote:

Daniel Marsh
Class 214 May 14 2003

Just Me and That's All

I would not like to be someone else. I would just like to be myself. I know what I do in my life so that's one reason I want to be myself.

It is great to be me. I know what I do in my wonderful life. I do a fantastic job being myself.

I know the different classes I go to. I go to karate. I know the different katas I need to know so far.

I like being me. I do everything I put my mind to. I am who I choose to be!

I believe you start off knowing who you are and then forget it along the way. It's time to get back to the pure heart of your inner child… so you can simply be Just Me and That's All!

Week 2:

Maximize your Physical Energy

<u>Week 2 – PWR® Moves</u>

Welcome to Week 2! How are you doing with your PWR® Moves? Every week we're going to add on just a little bit. This week, as you learn more on how to maximize your physical energy, we will step up our Re-Fuel area.

1. **REFLECT.** Continue to reflect for at least *10 minutes a day.*

2. **FOCUS.** Continue tuning your mind with positive affirmations every day, at least three times a day.

3. **RE-FUEL.** More on the basics:

   a. **Sweat.** Increase your cardiovascular time to at least *15 minutes a day,* for the 6 days of our week.
   b. **Stretch.** Add at least *5 minutes a day* of stretching, for the 6 days of our week.
   c. **Strengthen.** Add at least *5 minutes a day* of strengthening, for the 6 days of our week.
   d. **Hydrate.** Continue to make water your drink of choice.
   e. **Eat for Energy.** Add more fruits and vegetables to your diet. Go to the supermarket and become familiar with some of the PWR® Foods on pages 58 and 59 you currently do not use. Buy at least one new item off the list to try.
   f. **Breathe Deeply.** Practice deep breathing every day, particularly if you are feeling anxiety or simply want to take control of your nervous system. See the techniques on page 74, and/or use the *Power Living®: Mini-Escapes* CD.

4. **CONNECT.** Continue seeking joy every day!

5. **RELEASE.** Every day, continue to let go of *one* bind – a thought, a thing, a commitment, a relationship, a debt, etc.

Give it your best. Log your Progress.

Week 2 - Progress Log

As you receive PWR® Moves each week, rate yourself daily in each area using a 1 – 5 scale (1 =not successful, 5 =very successful).

Action	Day7	Day8	Day9	Day10	Day11	Day12
REFLECT						
Reflect 10 min.						
FOCUS						
Affirmations						
RE-FUEL						
Sweat 15 min.						
Stretch 5 min.						
Strengthen 5 min.						
Hydrate 8 glasses						
Add PWR® Foods						
Breathe Deeply						
CONNECT						
Experience Joy						
RELEASE						
Release 1 Bind						

Accomplishments/Challenges/Notes to Self:

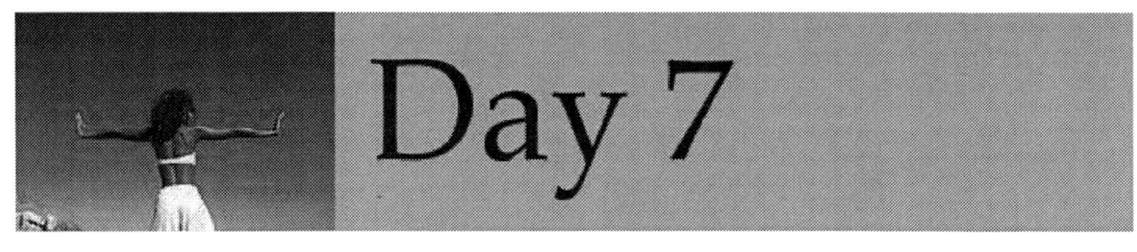

Eat to Live

"Tell me what you eat,
and I will tell you what you are."
- Anthelme Brillat-Savarin

Now that you have an overview of the Five Principles of Power Living®, and have gotten started on some of the primary habits, let's delve deeper this week into your body's performance.

I've found that it's good to start making adjustments to physical behavior early in the Practice because you can feel an *immediate* effect on your energy level. This can motivate you to continue making the other, more subtle, changes.

You are *what* and *how* you eat. When you eat whole foods in a conscious manner, you can heal and transform your body and mind. **"The 7 Rules of PWR® Eating"** can guide you. They are summarized in one simple motto:

**Eat variety in season, for a good reason;
in smart combinations, no imitations;
in moderation and without deprivation.**

Let me break it down:

1. **Eat Variety** – This is the best way to obtain enough protein, carbohydrates, fat and micronutrients. Make it colorful, and never eliminate an entire food category.

2. **In Season** – Choosing foods in season allows you to be in harmony with the environment and the cycles of nature. Fruits and vegetables in season are also cheaper, and taste better because of their shorter commute!

3. **For a Good Reason** – Know *why* you're eating. Make sure it's to re-fuel the body, instead of for emotional reasons. Try not to eat when you are angry, tired or lonely.

4. **In Smart Combinations** – Respect the chemical properties of each food and how certain foods react when combined. Bring order to your eating by having the easier to digest foods first. To avoid a traffic jam in your stomach, don't mix foods of different densities like proteins and starches.

5. **No Imitations** – Go for the real thing as Nature provided, whole, free of chemical additives, colorings and preservatives. Organically grown is the best if possible. Your body is intelligent; don't give it dumbed-down food!

6. **In Moderation** – We tend to bite off more than we can chew, literally! Don't stuff the pipes. If you put too much gas in a car, it will overflow. Use the same principle with the body. Give it smaller amounts of premium fuel so that it can perform most efficiently.

7. **Without Deprivation** – Make sure the food is delicious and satisfying. Use salt sparingly and spices soulfully. If you really have a craving for a cookie, go for it. But have *one* instead of the whole box!

Become familiar with the following list of PWR® Foods. Over the next few weeks we will be referring back to it. Always remember that certain foods that are good for one person may not have the same effect on another person. Through food experimenting, our goal is to come up with "My PWR® Foods" on page 188 – foods which really make *you* feel good and provide sustainable energy.

PWR® Foods

Fruits – Level 1			
Acid Fruits		**Sub-Acid Fruits**	
Cranberries	Lemons	Apples	Mangos
Grapefruits	Limes	Apricots	Nectarines
Kiwis	Pineapples	All Other Berries	Peaches
Oranges	Strawberries	Cherries	Pears
Tangerines	Tamarinds	Grapes	Plums
Sweet Fruits		**Melons**	
Bananas	Persimmons	Cantaloupe	Christmas
Dates	Plantains	Casaba	Honeydew
Dried Fruits	Prunes	Crenshaw	Watermelon
Figs	Raisins	Juan Canary	Pepino Melon

Vegetables – Level 2			
Onion	Kale	Spinach	String Beans
Garlic	Cucumber	Tomatoes	Eggplant
Celery	Peppers	Sprouts	Leafy Greens
Okra	Cabbage	Shallots	Beets
Radish	Scallion	Zucchini	Lettuce
Artichoke	Mushrooms	Sea Vegetables	Bamboo Shoots

Legumes – Level 3			
Chickpeas	Lima Beans	Kidney Beans	Navy Beans
Tofu	White Beans	Adzuki Beans	Pinto Beans
Lentils	Split peas	Black-eyed peas	Red Beans
Tempeh	Edamame	Soybeans	Broad Beans

Starches – Level 4			
Whole Grains		**Starchy Vegetables**	
Brown Rice	Buckwheat	Sweet Potatoes	Winter Squash
Amaranth	Kamut	Carrots	Broccoli
Millet	Spelt	Turnips	Cauliflower
Barley	Quinoa	Parsnips	Peas
Oats	Sprouted Breads	Rutabaga	Asparagus
Rice Cakes	Whole Grain Pasta	Corn	Brussels sprouts

Proteins – Level 5			
Poultry		**Meat***	
Chicken	Turkey Bacon	Beef	Venison
Turkey	Cornish Game Hen	Lamb	Veal
Duck	Omega-3 Eggs	Goat	Elk
Fish			
Salmon	Herring	Grouper	Whitefish
Tuna	Snapper	Sea Bass	Pompano
Trout	Haddock	Mackerel	Mahi-mahi
Halibut	Sole	Cod	Wahoo
Nuts and Seeds			
Almonds	Sunflower Seeds	Flaxseed	Hempseed
Tahini	Pumpkin Seeds	Almond Butter	Walnuts
Pecans	Hazelnuts	Macadamia	Brazil nuts
Dairy			
Goat's Milk**	Plain Yogurt	Plain Kefir	Hard Cheese
Goat Cheese	Plain Sour Cream	Ricotta Cheese	Cottage Cheese

Oils and Fats – Level 6			
Olive Oil	Coconut Oil	Hempseed Oil	Peanut Oil
Olives	Flaxseed Oil	Butter	Avocado

Condiments			
Ginger	Wasabi	Tamari	Amino Acids
Celtic Sea Salt	Herbs & Spices	Pickled Ginger	Mustard
Umeboshi Paste	Organic Flavoring Extracts	Apple Cider Vinegar	Natural Hot Sauce

Sweeteners			
Raw Honey	Natural Apple Sauce	Maple Syrup	Fruit Juice
Natural Jellies	Brown Rice Syrup	Agave Nectar	Stevia

Beverages			
Herbal Tea	100% Fresh Juices	Purified Water	Almond Milk
Rice Milk	100% Coconut Water	Organic Coffee	Oat Milk

* *I am not a huge proponent of meat, but if you eat it make sure it's lean, clean & organic.*

** *Be aware that many people are lactose-intolerant particularly to cow's milk and cheeses. Experiment and see what works for you. Goat's milk/cheese is often more easily tolerated.*

Reality Check

Today we're focused on **PWR® Eating**. How did you do with the Daily Lifestyle Log? Ask yourself:

Which of "The 7 Rules of PWR® Eating" do I currently follow?

What percent of my current diet is made up of PWR® Foods?

Which PWR® Foods do I want to include in my diet?

Which foods in my diet will I substitute for PWR® Foods?

Remember to stretch for at least 5 minutes today.

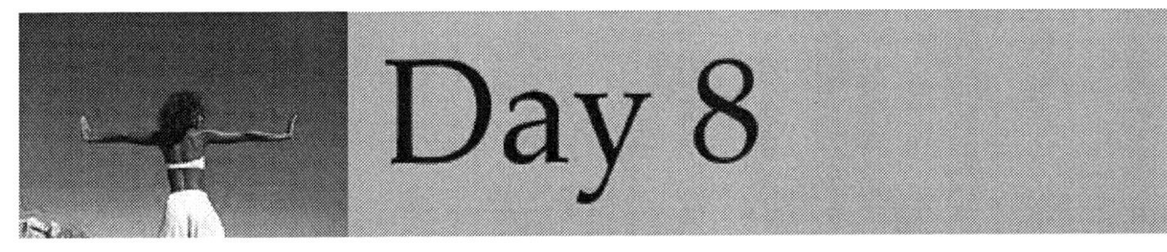

Power Up Your Meal!

"True happiness is impossible without true health and true health is impossible without a rigid control of the palate."
- Mahatma Gandhi

Research has documented the clear connection between our highly processed, "super-sized," Standard American Diet (S.A.D.), and the rise of certain modern degenerative diseases like diabetes, heart disease and cancer. In many ways, our ancestors who ate a more natural diet were better off than we are now.

By following "The 7 Rules of PWR® Eating," you can get back to the basics. As you can see from the list of PWR® Foods, there are a lot of items from which to choose.

Make Smart Combinations

Since I almost died from a digestive disorder, I pay a lot of attention to the gastrointestinal system. In fact, how to eat for optimum digestion has become one of my holistic health counseling specialties.

The levels on the PWR® Foods chart represent the digestibility of the various food groups and the preferred order in which they should be eaten. Here are some basic rules of food combining:

1. **Do not eat proteins (Level 5) and starches (Level 4) together.** Acid and alkaline properties neutralize each other. Most

protein foods require an acid base in the stomach in order to digest. Starches require an alkaline base. Proteins and starches combine well with non-starchy vegetables, but they do not combine well with each other.

2. **Legumes (Level 3) may be combined with Whole Grains (in Level 4) to make a complete protein.** Therefore, if you find you have a protein (such as chicken) and starch (such as rice) add a legume (such as black beans) and it will all be digested as complete protein.

3. **It is best to eat from *one* protein group at a time** (unless it's complementary as in the above example). Dairy, meat, egg and nut proteins, in particular, all require their own mix of enzymes for digestion. Including them together is likely to exhaust the digestive system.

4. **Eat only four to five different vegetables or fruits at one meal.** Don't overtax the digestive process.

5. **Do not mix fruit with proteins, starches, or any kind of vegetable.** Since fruits digest so quickly, they will rot and ferment in your stomach if you combine them with other food. There are some exceptions, like pineapple with dairy.

6. **Eat the sweet fruits and melons by themselves.** Don't combine them with each other, or with acid/sub-acid fruits.

7. **Use fats and oils (Level 6) sparingly.** They combine with everything except fruits; however, they slow down digestion.

8. **Drink *before* or *after* eating.** Drinking *during* a meal dilutes stomach acids prolonging digestion. If you must drink sip, don't gulp! Try to wait 30 minutes after eating before drinking.

9. **Don't eat 2 to 3 hours before bed.** Allow your food to digest and the body to burn fat.

These are some principles I learned very early on and then realized the health benefits later. Digestion plays a critical role in the healing process of the body. According to the Centers for Disease Control and Prevention (CDC), there are over 35 million visits to office-based physicians for digestive symptoms. Many of those visits can be eliminated by simply making smart food combinations.

Avoid a "Black-out"

You may notice a few things missing from the PWR® Foods list. Below is an overview of **PWR® Drainers** - foods you should limit or eliminate altogether. The best strategy is to simply "crowd-out" the PWR® Drainers by eating more PWR® Foods. Over time, your body will feel so great it will only crave good food.

PWR® Drainers

Unhealthy Fats		
Margarine	Fried Foods	Hydrogenated Oil
Lard	Fatty Meats	Solid Vegetable Shortening
Whole Milk	Roasted Nuts	Corn, Sunflower or Safflower Oil
High-Stress Sweets		
Refined Sugar	Corn Syrup	Artificial Coloring or Sweeteners
Hard Candy	Fructose	Canned fruits in syrup
Saccharin	Sucralose	Aspartame
Refined Carbohydrates		
White Rice	Pastries	Processed baked goods
White Flour	Instant Oatmeal	Dried Sugary Cereals
Beverages		
Soda & Coffee	Fruit Drinks	Chlorinated tap water

Laying out the adverse effects of unhealthy fats, high-stress sweets, refined carbohydrates, sugary and highly caffeinated drinks, is an entire book of its own - so I won't go into it here. Suffice it to say, these items will zap your energy and set the stage for disease. On the next page, I've included "A Day of Power Living®" Sample Meal Plan.

A Day of Power Living®

Sample Meal Plan

On Rising:	Cup of hot purified water with lemon Green Drink with Wheat Grass, Barley, etc.
Breakfast: (1 hr later)	Smoothie with Kefir, Pineapple, Ginger Hot Brown Rice Cereal Mix with Rice Milk
Break:	Sliced Apple Red Clover Tea
Lunch:	Mixed Green Salad with Olive Oil and Lemon with Grilled Chicken Breast or Boiled Egg
Break:	Mix Raisins, Almonds, Walnuts, Sunflower Seeds Peppermint Tea
Dinner:	Kale Chili with Seasonal Vegetables Long Brown Rice
Break:	Chamomile Tea

Note: If you signed up for the interactive element online, the above recipes will be sent via the weekly coaching emails. If you are interested in additional menus, recipes and more on "The 7 Rules of PWR® Eating," check out the "Seven-Day PWR® Detox" program, join one of our nutritional coaching sessions, and/or look for one of our upcoming Power Living® cookbooks.

Reality Check

Today we're focused on **food combining**. Ask yourself:

How many of the food combining rules do I currently follow?

What percent of my current diet is made up of PWR® Drainers?

Which food combinations do I want to include in my diet?

Which PWR® Drainers will I "crowd-out"?

Remember to sample a new PWR® Food today.

Practice Moderation

"Gluttony is an emotional escape,
a sign something is eating us."
- Peter De Vries

In a society of such excess, to preach moderation seems like blasphemy. Advertising, particularly for fast food restaurants, tempt us to "super-size" our fries and go for a "whopper" of a meal! With drive-up windows at many locales, our cars have become moving dinner tables. Sitting down to eat at home with the family seems like a thing of the past.

When it comes to food, *how* and *how much* you eat is just as important as *what* you eat. Here are some basic principles:

- **Use smaller dishes and utensils.** The plate will look full and the portions will be more reasonable.
- **Give thanks for the meal**. This helps put you in a peaceful frame of mind. Take a deep breath before the first bite.
- **Slow down.** Chew thoroughly before swallowing, and put your fork down between mouthfuls. The *process* of eating affects digestion and satisfaction.
- **Don't take seconds.** Keep serving dishes off the table.
- **Pause in the middle of the meal.** It takes 20 minutes to feel full, so check in with the body before you continue eating.

Make meal-time sacred. When you savor the experience your body will reward you with better digestion and robust health.

Size Matters

Although you shouldn't obsess about them, calories *do* count. It's been said that we, on average, can survive on one-third of our daily food intake. If that's the case, many of us are eating for three! Unless you are about to have twins, it's time to reign in the portions. Here are a few guidelines:

Portions	
1 ounce cheese	a pair of dice
3 ounces of meat, fish or poultry	a deck of cards
1 serving salad dressing	1 Tablespoon or size of thumb
1 serving fruit or vegetables	½ cup or a tennis ball
1 serving pasta or cereal	½ cup or size of a fist
1 serving peanut/almond butter	1 Tablespoon or size of walnut
1 serving bread	a cassette tape
1 serving nuts	a handful

Restaurant servings are generally 3 to 4 times normal serving sizes. Consider taking at least half of your meal home or share it with someone. Another option is to order an appetizer or side dish. Also, look out for hidden sugar and salt in condiments.

Give your Body a Break

Your body does a lot of work to keep you functioning. Below are two ways to honor your body:

- **Eat Multiple Small Meals.** Eat small meals approximately every 3 hours. This keeps your energy up.

- **Fast One Day a Week.** There are many different types of fasts – from all liquids to fruits in the morning and vegetables in the afternoon. The main goal is to give your body a rest and allow it to detoxify itself.

If you are kind to your body, it will repay you in so many wonderful ways. Your spirit will also feel lighter.

<u>Reality Check</u>

Today we're focused on **<u>moderation</u>**. Ask yourself:

What snacks from the PWR® Foods list will I add to my diet?

____

____

____

What changes do I want to make to my mealtime to have a more satisfying and easeful experience?

____

____

____

____

What times will I eat for more sustainable energy?

____

____

____

Remember to experience joy today.

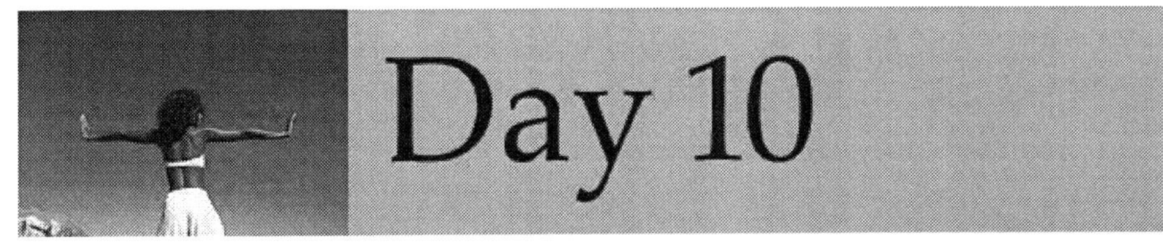

Exercise to Energize

"After dinner, rest awhile, after supper, walk a mile."
- Arabic Proverb

I love to eat! Thank goodness, I also love to exercise. The two go hand-in-hand for optimum health, with the other pieces being adequate sleep and breath control. These are the basics; nothing too complicated. My philosophy on exercise is also very simple:

Every day you must sweat, stretch and strengthen.

Let me break that down:

1. **Sweat** – Exercise is considered "cardiovascular" when it elevates your heart rate to 60 to 85 percent of its maximum rate. Basically, you need to sweat for about 30 minutes and still be able to talk! This will strengthen your heart and lungs, as well as burn calories and lower body fat.

2. **Stretch** – Stretching helps increase flexibility, reduce risk of injury, minimize muscle soreness, and improve overall performance. It's a good way to cool down after an aerobic activity, and be warmed up enough to strengthen.

3. **Strengthen** – Strength training is essential to boosting your metabolism and enhancing bone density. The more lean tissue you have the more body fat you will shed, even while you sleep! It also helps to improve posture, which will make you look better and age more gracefully.

The ratio I like to use is **30:15:15** – 30 minutes sweating, 15 minutes stretching, 15 minutes strengthening. That's a total of 60 minutes a day, 6 days a week. Obviously, we're working up to these numbers gradually in this program. Some forms of exercise, such as the yoga I teach, give you all of this and more in one session!

Go For Personality and Variety

Does this mean you have to hit the gym every day? No! There are a number of things you can do depending on your personality:

Exercise for your Personality			
Social/Playful	**Competitive**	**Worker**	**Peaceful/Solo**
Dancing	Tennis	Gardening	Swimming
Aerobics Class	Racquetball	Mowing the Lawn	Running
Cycling	Basketball	Carpentry	Yoga/Tai Chi
Skating	Volleyball	Washing the Car	Martial Arts
Skiing	Soccer	Housework	Golf

Some of the above activities provide more cardiovascular benefits than others, so make sure to vary your workouts. Variety also prevents your body from adapting which will eventually prompt it to stop burning as many calories. Not only vary the days you do certain exercises, vary your speed. In other words, train in intervals – 2 minutes walking at 5 mph, then 2 minutes at 7 mph, etc. If you don't want to do push-ups or use a weight machine, add light dumbbells to your cardio workout.

Prepare for Performance

As with anything, planning is important in your exercise strategy:

- **Schedule** - Reserve a time slot each day for exercise. Have your workout clothes handy and ready-to-go.
- **Eat** - Eat a small meal 2 hours before exercise, and eat within 2 hours after exercise.
- **Drink** – Drink at least one glass of purified water before and after your workout, and every 10 - 15 minutes during.

Reality Check

Today we're focused on **exercise**. Answer the following:

What is my exercise personality? What activities do I enjoy?

____

____

How and when will I *sweat*?

____

____

How and when will I *stretch*?

____

____

How and when will I *strengthen*?

____

____

What will I eat before and after exercise?

____

Remember to sweat for at least 15 minutes today.

Use Breath as a Change Agent

"Controlling the breath,
is a prerequisite to controlling the mind and body."
- Swami Rama

The word spirit comes from the Latin word "spiritus" which means breath. In many cultures, breath is seen as a portal to the soul – the connection to life and earth, and God. In fact, breath is life. Life begins with the first breath and ends with the last. The average person can go without food for several weeks, without liquid for several days. But if you close off the oxygen supply to your brain for four minutes, you could die.

Breathing is the only automatic vital life function you can voluntarily control, deliberately affecting the autonomic nervous system, as well as emotions. Breath can be used to:

- build energy
- focus the mind
- aid in weight loss
- help manage pain
- change your mood
- lower blood pressure
- heal physical problems
- control the "fight-or-flight" stress response

Are you using the full potential of your lungs? Probably not! In one day, you take about 20,000 breaths. Everyone breathes, but not everyone takes in the same amount of oxygen. Learning to harness the breath is one of the most powerful things you can do. A five percent increase in your breath capacity can increase the efficiency of your body a thousand-fold. If you take time to learn how to breathe *effectively*, you will improve the quality of your entire life.

Protect your Lungs

Pollution from particulate matter, such as pollen, dust and mold can irritate the eyes, throat and lungs. Consider purchasing an air filter as a protective strategy. It is also smart to have house plants throughout your home to absorb any carbon dioxide and toxic chemicals from the air and increase the oxygen flow. Plants act as a natural purification system.

Here's where I must also mention smoking. I'm not going to preach, but I will remind you of the top-line effects of smoking on your health *just in case* you engage in the habit.

- Tobacco use remains the leading *preventable* cause of death in the U.S., causing emphysema, heart disease, strokes, and cancer.
- Smoking cigarettes for as few as five years can have a permanent effect on the lungs, the heart, the eyes, the throat, the urinary tract, the digestive organs, the bones and joints, and the skin – even if the smoker quits.
- Someone who smokes a pack or more of cigarettes a day lives 7 years less on average than someone who never smoked.

Despite irreversible effects of smoking, many studies prove that tobacco-related health effects decline substantially as time away from smoking increases – so the time to quit is now!

Breathing Techniques

Breath is the life force (*prana*) and energy (*ki*) that moves through your body. Here are three simple, yet powerful breath techniques you can do anywhere, at any time. Make sure to sit or stand with your spine held tall. These techniques can be done separately, or one following the next.

- **Breath Awareness.** Begin to focus on your breathing, without trying to change it. Simply notice where you are right in this moment. Feel the sensation of inspiration, the process of drawing air into the lungs. Allow your breath to be the gateway to the Present. Observe for at least 30 seconds.
- **Transformational Breath.** Begin to consciously direct the breath, inhaling and exhaling through the nose. The nose is a more efficient respiration agent than the mouth. It filters, moisturizes, warms and directs the airflow. As you inhale, fill your abdomen with energy and oxygen. As you exhale, release fully all tension and toxins. Inhale positive affirming thoughts, exhale all negative limiting thoughts. Inhale strength. Exhale fear. Inhale confidence. Exhale self-doubt. Inhale the Present. Exhale the past. Wherever you are, you can use your breath to transform your state of mind and body.
- **Deep Three-Part Breath.** To begin, exhale fully through the nose. Then, to inhale, expand first the abdomen, then feel the air flowing up to expand the lower ribs and upper chest. Exhale from the upper chest, feeling the collarbones lower, then relax the lower ribs and gently pull in the abdomen to empty the lungs as fully as possible. Continue letting the three parts blend into the next, so the breath is one continuous, smooth flow. Breathe slowly and deeply for 1 to 3 minutes. After your last exhalation, return the breath to normal and observe how you feel. This deep, diaphragmatic breathing is very calming for the nervous system and can take in seven times more oxygen than in shallow, chest breathing.

Reality Check

Today we're focused on **breath**. Answer the following:

When I inhale, does my abdomen go IN or OUT? Place your hand on your abdomen and find out.

☐ IN ☐ OUT

Next time you see a baby or dog sleeping – notice how the belly *expands* when they inhale and *releases* when they exhale. That's our natural flow of breath. If you are breathing in the opposite way, don't despair – with practice you can reverse the flow.

What does my breath tell me about my state of mind? You can use your breath as a signal to spot anxiety. Do you ever find your breath becoming shallow and rapid? If so, when does this happen?

____

____

____

I will use the breath techniques in the following situations:

____

____

____

Remember to drink at least 8 glasses of purified water today.

Make Sleep Sacred

"Rest is not a matter of doing absolutely nothing.
Rest is repair."
- Daniel W. Josselyn

A vital energy source, sleep is the time when the body heals and the mind assimilates the learning from the day. It is as important as food and air. Quantity and quality are key. According to a CNN survey, one out of three American adults experience sleep problems ranging from snoring to narcolepsy. Ask yourself:

- Do I often feel irritable?
- Do I remember my dreams?
- Do I have problems concentrating?
- Do I sleep eight hours and still feel tired?
- Do I wake up extremely hungry and can't seem to feel satisfied after I eat?

A chronic lack of rapid-eye-movement (REM) sleep can reduce productivity, increase stress, induce irritability, and lead to depression and disease. Lack of sleep can also sabotage any attempt to lose weight since certain hormones are affected by sleep. According to recent studies, when you don't get enough sleep, it drives the *leptin* levels down, which means you don't feel as satisfied after you eat. Lack of sleep also causes *ghrelin* levels to rise, which means your appetite is stimulated, so you want more food. The two combined can set the stage for overeating, which in turn may lead to weight gain.

Set the Stage for Sleep

Although there is no one formula for how much sleep is enough, most adults need between 7 to 8 hours of *uninterrupted* sleep a night. You should wake up refreshed in the morning without the use of an alarm clock and feel energetic all day. Reasons for not sleeping well could include:

- noise
- bodily pain
- a cluttered bedroom
- anxiety or an overactive mind
- disturbance from your partner
- an uncomfortable bed and/or sheets
- excessive stimulation from drugs or caffeine

To live your most productive life, make sleep a priority. Create habits and an environment that is conducive to rest:

- **Regularity.** Go to sleep and wake up at the same time. Use the bedroom to sleep; no TV watching or work.
- **Good Energy.** If you must use a clock, wake up to soft music instead of a buzzer. Use a clock with batteries. Remove electric clock radios from close to your bed since they can disturb your own electromagnetic field.
- **Peaceful State.** Stay away from caffeine, nicotine and alcohol at least 4 to 6 hours before bed. Exercise regularly - but not too close to bedtime. If you must eat something close to bedtime, eat foods high in tryptophan, such as bananas. Have chamomile tea to calm the body.
- **Comfort.** Make sure the bed is comfortable and your room uncluttered, dark and quiet. Use lavender as a calming scent. Soft music and candles can also induce peace.

With a good night's sleep, you will have better relationships, perform daily tasks more efficiently, and have the energy to pursue your divine destiny.

Reality Check

Today we're focused on **sleep**. Answer the following:

How much uninterrupted sleep do I get a night? ____________

Is this enough to wake up refreshed and energetic, without using coffee or other sources of caffeine? __________

What are some potential impediments to my getting a good night's rest? (Look at the list on page 77)

____

____

____

____

____

What can I do to make the situation better?

____

____

____

____

Remember to practice deep breathing today.

A PWR® Moment

A Walk in the Piazza

The Power of Balanced Living

My Mom, Janie Sykes-Kennedy, got into holistic health and yoga in the early '70's. We even had an industrial wheat grass juicer! I knew all of the principles of healthy living at a very young age. Despite that, I wasn't always the yogini with six-pack abs.

I grew up a somewhat chubby child. My family never called me fat; just "big-boned." My sister was the skinny one. My weight always seemed to fluctuate until I lived in Rome to study design. There, I was drawing every day and absolutely in love with the culture. I went to the piazza in the mornings to buy fresh food and walked everywhere. When I returned to the United States, my perspective on life was more balanced and my body stabilized. I even started modeling.

I had gotten back to the basics - moving every day, eating a variety of whole foods, and having joy in my life. It wasn't about a diet; it was about creating a sustainable lifestyle. Later, when I hit the corporate world, I allowed myself to get off-balance which led to my illness. I had to find my joy again and understand that being healthy is a *daily* practice of tuning the mind, nurturing the body and feeding the spirit.

Week 3:

Align your Spiritual Energy

Week 3 – PWR® Moves

You made it to Week 3! Are you getting used to your PWR® Moves? How's the PWR® Food? This week, we're going to continue stepping up our Re-Fuel area. Also, as you learn more on how to align you spiritual energy, we're going to add more reflection time.

1. **REFLECT.** Increase your reflection time to at least *15 minutes a day* – adding 5 minutes to your morning time.

2. **FOCUS.** Continue tuning your mind with positive affirmations every day, at least three times a day.

3. **RE-FUEL.** More on the basics:

   a. **Sweat.** Increase your cardiovascular time to at least *20 minutes a day*, for the 6 days of our week.
   b. **Stretch.** Increase stretching to at least *10 minutes a day*, for the 6 days of our week.
   c. **Strengthen.** Continue strengthening for at least *5 minutes a day*, for the 6 days of our week.
   d. **Hydrate.** Continue to make water your drink of choice.
   e. **Eat for Energy.** Continue to add PWR® Foods to your diet. See what PWR® Drainers you can begin to "crowd-out."
   f. **Breathe Deeply.** Continue to practice deep breathing.
   g. **Sleep Soundly.** Focus on getting a minimum of 7 hours of sleep a night – or whatever you have determined is your optimum level.

4. **CONNECT.** Continue seeking joy every day!

5. **RELEASE.** Every day, continue to let go of *one* bind – a thought, a thing, a commitment, a relationship, a debt, etc.

Give it your best. Log your Progress.

Week 3 - Progress Log

As you receive PWR® Moves each week, rate yourself daily in each area using a 1 – 5 scale (1 =not successful, 5 =very successful).

Action	Day13	Day14	Day15	Day16	Day17	Day18
REFLECT						
Reflect 15 min.						
FOCUS						
Affirmations						
RE-FUEL						
Sweat 20 min.						
Stretch 10 min.						
Strengthen 5 min.						
Hydrate 8 glasses						
Add PWR® Foods						
Breathe Deeply						
Sleep Soundly						
CONNECT						
Experience Joy						
RELEASE						
Release 1 Bind						

Accomplishments/Challenges/Notes to Self:

____

____

____

____

____

Day 13

Assess your Gifts

"Have the daring to accept yourself as a bundle of possibilities, and undertake the game of making the most of your best. "
- Harry Emerson Fosdick

Now that we've laid the groundwork for the physical habits, let's go back to laying the spiritual foundation: **Live on Purpose.**

Passion is often an indicator of Purpose. Passion is something you have deep inside you – a desire, a dream. Honoring that passion is essential to your joy and prosperity. It allows you to be true to your heart, living a life that *feels* right. If you deny your passion, you're selling your Self – as well as your loved ones - short. Ask:

- What do I enjoy doing most?
- What comes completely natural to me?
- What do I do that adds distinctive value?
- What do I look forward to doing more than anything else?

Don't let fear of failure, or success, hold you back from experiencing life and reaching your divine destiny. If you repress your inborn desires, you're at great risk of diminishing your God-given talents and living a spiritually anorexic life full of regrets. NOW is the time to pursue what captures your heart. Don't die "with your music still inside." Do what makes your heart sing. Be honest with your Self. Take time to identify your passions through a systematic process of self-assessment.

God Wants to Use You Up!

People used to always comment about my seemingly divergent interests. I would create a financial model in Excel, just as easily as I would paint. I worked at Harvard Business School as a Research Associate, while I modeled on the side. At one point I believed I had to choose between my left-brain and right-brain tendencies to be taken seriously. As a result, I abandoned my painting and modeling, as I became more immersed in business.

Now, *all* aspects of my experience and personality are being used to further my Purpose. Every single thing I've done previously has prepared me to manifest The Power Living® Practice to share with you today. How amazing is that?

> "For I am already being poured out like a drink offering, and the time has come for my departure."
> - 2 Timothy 4:6

In the same way, every single part of YOU will be used when you are *on Purpose*… the triumphs and the trials. God wants to use you up… pour you out like a drink offering. Nothing wasted!

Your Thorn in the Flesh

Your struggle may lead to your greatest success. That very thing that you've battled with or had to overcome may become a part of your personal mission. That has proven true for me: transforming from the stressed-out executive to a holistic health expert! Who would have thought I would be counseling people about life balance and healthy living? Yet, who better to do so? I've been through the fire and lived to tell about it. Ask yourself:

- What is my story?
- What struggles may add color to my own Purpose?
- What have I learned along the way that may help someone else?

Reality Check

Today we're focused on **passion and divine gifts**.

What is my passion? What would you do with your life if you had no limits of time or money?

____

____

____

What are my natural gifts and strengths?

1. ____

2. ____

3. ____

4. ____

5. ____

What is my "thorn in the flesh" and how can it help others?

____

____

Remember to stretch for at least 10 minutes today.

Day 14

Define your Core

"He who stands for nothing falls for anything."
- Unknown

From a sociological standpoint, values are defined as the relatively enduring beliefs that serve as guides for what is considered "appropriate" behavior and are widely accepted by the members of society. Therein is our challenge. *Who decides what is appropriate and acceptable?* Now it's time for you to create your own definition of success and design your own life. It starts with your core values. Ask yourself:

- What drives my life?
- What is important to *me*?
- Do my daily actions reflect my core beliefs?
- What values have I inherited that don't serve me anymore?

Your values are the lens through which you see the world. They are the beliefs or attitudes about what is good, right, worthwhile, and important in life. They form the foundation of your character. Some values refer to how you should act such as be honest or disciplined. Other values refer to what you want to obtain such as security or wisdom. The ranking of your values form your value system. Once you have a clear sense of your own standards, you will be able to allocate your energy more effectively, make more authentic decisions, and move further along the path to your destiny.

Live from the Inside Out

Lack of awareness of the values that are at the core of who you are, clouds your vision and makes you vulnerable to external forces. You are liable to "sway with the wind" – lacking true conviction and passion about anything. You end up leading your life from the outside in rather than the inside out.

Having a life direction and clear personal priorities to which you are committed, prevents you from drifting aimlessly. It forms the basis for the skills and habits you choose to develop, and the life decisions you make. A strong sense of your values also builds high self-esteem – one of the key indicators to success.

Watch Out for a Head-On Collision!

Your values determine your priorities - where you spend your time, and how you think and behave. If you value your health, you are likely to workout instead of watch TV. If you value financial security, you are likely to invest extra money instead of buy a new car.

At times, however, your values may conflict with each other and need to be managed. Many of our beliefs are formed as we grow up - through family, cultural, religious and schooling influences.

> "We never know the worth of water 'til the well is dry."
> - English Proverb

This lifetime of conditioning may not synch with who you are now causing a subconscious layer of stress. For example, working late until a job is done versus spending the evening with loved ones. Often you may not realize this disconnect until a crisis occurs – such as a panic attack, illness, death or divorce. It's SO much easier to *know* who you are… and then *be* who you are!

<u>Reality Check</u>

Today we're focused on **<u>values</u>**. Take time to do a personal values audit. Actively *choose* the core values you want to live by - get rid of the *"shoulds"*. Look at the Core Values Worksheet on pages 89 - 91. Rank each value (as "A", "B", "C"). Then, choose your top five from group "A".

Transfer your top 5 values to this sheet.

My core values are:

1. ____

2. ____

3. ____

4. ____

5. ____

<u>What do I have to change to live my core values?</u>

____

____

____

____

Remember to "crowd-out" a PWR® Drainer today.

Core Values Worksheet

From this list of values, select the five that are most important to you - as guides for how to behave, or as components of a valued way of life. Feel free to add any values of your own to this list.

Value	Definition	Rank
Acceptance	to be accepted as I am	
Accuracy	to be accurate in my opinions and beliefs	
Achievement	to have important accomplishments	
Adventure	to have new and exciting experiences	
Attractiveness	to be physically attractive	
Authority	to be in charge of and responsible for others	
Autonomy	to be self-determined and independent	
Beauty	to appreciate beauty around me	
Caring	to take care of others	
Challenge	to take on difficult tasks and problems	
Change	to have a life full of change and variety	
Comfort	to have a pleasant and comfortable life	
Commitment	to make enduring, meaningful commitments	
Compassion	to feel and act on concern for others	
Contribution	to make a lasting contribution in the world	
Cooperation	to work collaboratively with others	
Courtesy	to be considerate and polite toward others	
Creativity	to have new and original ideas	
Dependability	to be reliable and trustworthy	
Ecology	to live in harmony with the environment	
Excitement	to have a life full of thrills and stimulation	
Faithfulness	to be loyal and true in relationships	
Fame	to be known and recognized	
Family	to have a happy, loving family	
Fitness	to be physically fit and strong	
Flexibility	to adjust to new circumstances easily	
Forgiveness	to be forgiving of others	
Friendship	to have close, supportive friends	
Fun	to play and have fun	
Generosity	to give what I have to others	

Value	Definition	Rank
Genuineness	to act in a manner that is true to who I am	
God's Will	to seek and obey the will of God	
Growth	to keep changing and growing	
Health	to be physically well and healthy	
Helpfulness	to be helpful to others	
Honesty	to be honest and truthful	
Hope	to maintain a positive and optimistic outlook	
Humility	to be modest and unassuming	
Humor	to see the humorous side of myself & the world	
Independence	to be free from dependence on others	
Industry	to work hard and well at my life tasks	
Inner Peace	to experience personal peace	
Intimacy	to share my innermost experiences with others	
Justice	to promote fair and equal treatment for all	
Knowledge	to learn and contribute valuable knowledge	
Leisure	to take time to relax and enjoy	
Loved	to be loved by those close to me	
Loving	to give love to others	
Mastery	to be competent in my everyday activities	
Mindfulness	to live conscious/mindful of the Present moment	
Moderation	to avoid excesses and find a middle ground	
Monogamy	to have one close, loving relationship	
Non-conformity	to question and challenge authority and norms	
Nurturance	to take care of and nurture others	
Openness	to be open to new experiences and ideas	
Order	to have a life that is well-ordered and organized	
Passion	to have deep feelings re: ideas, activities, people	
Pleasure	to feel good	
Popularity	to be well-liked by many people	
Position Power	to have control over others	
Prosperity	to have abundance and success	
Purpose	to have meaning and direction in my life	
Rationality	to be guided by reason and logic	
Realism	to see and act realistically and practically	

Value	Definition	Rank
Responsibility	to make and carry out responsible decisions	
Risk	to take risks and chances	
Romance	to have intense, exciting love in my life	
Safety	to be safe and secure	
Self-acceptance	to accept my Self as I am	
Self-control	to be disciplined in my own actions	
Self-esteem	to feel good about my Self	
Self-knowledge	to have a deep/honest understanding of my Self	
Service	to be of service to others	
Sexuality	to have an active and satisfying sex life	
Simplicity	to live life simply, with minimal needs	
Solitude	to have time and space to be with my Self	
Spirituality	to grow and mature spiritually	
Stability	to have a life that stays fairly consistent	
Tolerance	to accept and respect those who differ from me	
Tradition	to follow respected patterns of the past	
Virtue	to live a morally pure and excellent life	
World Peace	to work to promote peace in the world	

Note: Examine each value to ensure that it is an end value and not a means to an end. For example, wealth is seldom a value in itself. It's usually the means to status, power, security, recognition, freedom, pleasure, helping others, or some other end value.

Day 15

Adjust your Vision

"The man who has no imagination has no wings."
-- Muhammad Ali

Vision is the ability to see your future in your Present. It is the gift of seeing not just what *is*, but what *can be*. The ability to see in your heart what is currently invisible to the physical eyes is a powerful force. It is how new businesses and leaders are born. Vision can motivate, give direction, and guide decisions in your work, life, and ultimately, the world around you. Ask yourself:

- What do I *see* for my life?
- What may be clouding my sight?
- Am I serious about achieving my Purpose?
- How much time do I spend pursuing my divine path?

Many people have sight, but lack vision. They ignore the inspirations that are placed in their hearts, are consumed by the past, or are too busy with daily routine to see clearly. Often fear, short-term thinking, tradition and "conventional wisdom" creep in and cloud the picture. Instead of claiming their innate gifts, they give up and deny their destinies. Does this sound familiar?

If you want to be a visionary, instead of simply a daydreamer, invest time in understanding your own vision. Develop a *sense of urgency* in pursuit of your personal goals. The more you actively move towards your vision, the closer you will be to moving out of your current circumstances and toward the fulfillment of your Purpose.

See your Life

One skill to aid you in your success is the ability to *see* the positive outcome in your mind. Used therapeutically by doctors and psychologists since the early 1970s, visualization is the practice of creating a mental image of a situation in the way you would *like* it to happen. It can help you manage stress, perform at your peak, unleash creativity, and activate the body's self-healing processes. It is now used as an adjunct to conventional cancer treatment.

Researchers believe that visualization encourages activity in the right hemisphere of the brain, which sends a message to the autonomic nervous system. If visualization is repeated enough in detail, the individual begins to act as if the image were a reality. By mentally rehearsing an important event and seeing your Self achieve success, you also increase your confidence. Top athletes use the technique to improve their performance.

Note that visualization is different than visioning. Visioning is fueled by reflection and divine guidance; visualization is a tool to make the vision *feel* real to you.

> "See things as you would have them be instead of as they are."
> - Robert Collier

Clean your Lenses

Don't compare your Self with others. Starting right now, do not turn to others for validation. Instead, look through your own lenses. Seek confirmation from the Universe. Start building your own picture of your Self and your life. See and accept who you are at your Core, instead of looking to external things or people for your self-worth. And remember… everybody has their cross to bear. You don't know what is going on in another person's life. So, before you envy or judge – stop, take a breath and go inside! The grass is really *not* greener on the other side. The real work is there, right at *your* Core. Claim your own patch of land.

Reality Check

Today we're focused on **vision**.

What is my vision? Write a Personal Vision Statement reflecting your passions, natural strengths and core values.

What action can I take today to move me closer to my vision?

What are 5 things I want to *accomplish* in my lifetime?

1.

2.

3.

4.

5.

Remember to practice deep breathing today.

Day 16

Release Unbelief

"All things are possible to him who believes."
- Mark 9:23

Undoubtedly, once you declare your path, obstacles will come. If you're really looking deeply, you'll see that many of those roadblocks come from inside.

What prevents people from pursuing their heart's desire? Besides everyday busyness that precludes us from simply being still, I believe one key challenge for most people is *unbelief*. Unbelief in:

- a healthy body
- a peaceful heart
- the power of choice
- personal prosperity
- the fact that you deserve more
- your ability to live your absolute best life

There is a story in the Bible (Mark 9:14-24) about Jesus healing a demon-possessed boy. The boy was on the ground foaming at the mouth. Jesus asked the boy's father, "How long has he been like this?" "From childhood," he answered. "It has often thrown him into fire or water to kill him. But if you can do anything, take pity on us and help us." "*If* you can?" said Jesus. "Everything is possible for him who believes." Immediately the boy's father exclaimed, "I do believe, help me overcome my unbelief!"

In your heart, your Core Self *knows* you're special. You know you were created for a Purpose and have unique talents to share. The basic belief is there. Over time, however, layers of doubt and fear may have covered that belief moving you into a state of unbelief. This is evident when I ask clients to share their dreams:

- "If I could, I would have a healthy relationship."
- "If I could, I would have my own business."
- "If I could, I would lose weight."

IF you can? I am here to say that you *can* overcome your unbelief.

Grow in Faith

Regardless of your religion, it's important to have faith. I'm talking about a belief in a power that is both *greater than* you and *in* you. It's a power that you can tap into by being conscious of it, believing in it and being with it.

Faith is a form of *knowing* which cannot be expressed in words, and can only be verified by experience. It is a belief in things not seen, implying an element of trust and an act of courage to leave your intellect behind. It requires humility and patience. It is like electricity. You can't see it, but you can see the light.

> "Faith is not something to grasp it is a state to grow into."
> - Mahatma Gandhi

Faith in a Higher Power will not only sustain you in challenging times, but it is also good for your life expectancy. A Dartmouth Medical School study found that those who derive strength and comfort from their spiritual faith are three times more likely to survive than those who don't. Those with faith generally have less fear, anxiety, and stress, all risk factors for disease.

Reality Check

Today we're focused on **unbelief and faith**.

What do I believe in? How would I describe my faith?

Where is my unbelief? What doubt is holding you back?

What action can I take today to deepen my faith and/or confront unbelief?

Remember to release one bind today.

Day 17

Appreciate Divine Timing

"To everything there is a season,
a time for every Purpose under Heaven."
- Ecclesiastes 3:1

Some apparent obstacles on the road to Purpose are divinely appointed. As my Mom says, "God is saving you from yourself!" That is her way of reminding me to "get out of the way", have patience, and let life's process unfold.

In a world of extreme makeovers and instant messages, we have been conditioned to expect immediate results. Like spoiled children, we often get upset when things don't happen according to our desired timetable. Are you impatient with the Universe?

- "I'm *not ready* to have a child now."
- "I'll miss this opportunity if the business deal doesn't close *right away*."

Some events may seem too early, or too late. In reality, life rarely happens in a precise, self-prescribed order, yet it usually happens right on time.

No Magic Wand

The Universe is here to support us, but it doesn't follow the magic-wand principle - wave it and the fairy godmother delivers. Like fruit, certain things need to ripen, and life's greatest joys are often the ones that are not charted. Having a long-term plan is necessary to achieve your life vision. However, it is important to realize that there may be some other items on the cosmic menu.

When you open your eyes to this fundamental truth, you will partake in an even greater feast than what you could have imagined. The key is to be able to *recognize* and *appreciate* divine timing – working with it instead of blocking its flow.

Active Waiting

Sometimes your desires may not sync with your Purpose, or there may be some lessons for you to learn to help you mature spiritually. If you're feeling frustrated, don't give up what's in your heart. Instead, detach your Self from a perfect schedule, and become a partner with providence. Be patient and learn from the lessons of unplanned detours. Trust the eternal rhythm of Life.

You can aid the process by sowing the seed or delay it by complaining that the gardener quit! Instead of resisting the flow through procrastination and worrying, engage in *active waiting* by preparing your Self for that desired outcome.

> "As the body without
> the spirit is dead,
> so faith without
> deeds is dead."
> - James 2:26

For example, if you are dreaming of starting your own business, begin to get your financial house in order. If you are yearning for the ideal mate, hone your own lifestyle habits. Patience and active waiting will reward you with healthier relationships, higher-quality work, and peace of mind. With practice the process actually becomes easier and you begin to trust that *Thy* Will Be Done is so much better than *My* Will Be Done! Why take the bus when your limo is coming?

Reality Check

Today we're focused on **divine timing**.

How has divine timing worked in my life?

____

____

____

____

____

____

In what areas do I need to "ease up" and let life flow?

____

____

____

____

____

____

Remember to sweat for at least 20 minutes today.

Day 18

Become a Human... Being

"Life is not measured by how many breaths we take,
but by the moments that take our breath away."
- Unknown

In a culture that places so much value on *doing*, sometimes it's not easy simply *to be*. We place a premium on *activity* and *efficiency*. Yet, continuous busyness can lead to lower productivity, and higher levels of disease. Ask yourself:

- What am I so busy doing?
- Am I living consciously in the moment?
- How often do I look at the clouds passing by in the sky?
- Am I giving the world ALL of me or an outdated model?

We are often more focused on the past or the future, than the Present. We tend to fill up any empty space with distractions. Operating on automatic pilot, we miss the very essence of life.

Develop Presence

When you think of the word *presence*, you may think of charisma. I'd like to take that further with the following definition:

Presence is being Present with your Purpose.

Presence is being fully here now sharing *all* of your Core. When you are living on Purpose and are fully Present, you emit an energy that attracts. It is unique because it is from within.

Many clients ask, "How can I even be Present *given all of the things I have to do*?" My answer is, "It's not an either-or situation. Be Present *with* the things you have to do. So you can actually *be* there!" Bring your Purpose to the table allowing it to guide your actions. Practice mindfulness by slowing down and being more intentional with ordinary tasks. Watch each moment. Relinquish any inner resistance and judgment to what is. If you are angry or sad, just observe the feeling.

Observation is the conscious act of being aware of any object, activity, process or phenomenon *in all its details using all senses*. Developing a keen ability to observe is an important skill. It can help close a business deal, deepen a relationship, and even save a life. Wherever you are, be totally there. It is only by being fully in this moment that the future moment might be one of greater clarity.

> "Observe the wonders as they occur around you. Don't claim them. Feel the artistry moving through and be silent."
> - Rumi

You Are Not Your Job

My clients who are newly-minted entrepreneurs often echo the same concern:

> "I sometimes don't want to go to networking events because my business is small. I usually end up talking about my old job so I sound legitimate."

Next time you're at a cocktail party and encounter a new face don't ask, "What do you *do*?" Instead ask, "Who *are* you?" Start getting into the habit of relating to a person's Core, and presenting your Self from your Core. You are more than your net worth or a job title. Develop a mindset of openness. Try not to judge your Self and others on appearances and titles, and experience the joy and peace of becoming a human… *being*.

Reality Check

Today we're focused on **Presence**.

Who Am I? Let's go back to our first Core question. If someone asked you, "Who are you?" how would your Core answer now?

Practice Mindfulness. Today, slow down and be more intentional with ordinary tasks. Watch each moment. Later in the day, write down your observations.

Remember to experience joy today.

A PWR® Moment

Respecting the Cosmic Chef

The Power of Divine Timing

Some time ago, after splitting with her boyfriend of six years, my sister declared that she was going to be happily single while she focused on running her computer software training company. And I truly believed she was.

As she grew her business, marriage was the furthest thing from her mind. Eighteen months after her declaration, a former boyfriend, from 12 years past, took her completely by surprise and asked her to marry him. After getting over the initial shock, my sister began to date him again and ten months later they got married.

The interesting note here is that he had asked her to marry him years ago when they first dated, but she did not feel they were ready. Now, after celebrating their second wedding anniversary, they agree that they did not have all the ingredients to make it work back then. If they had tried to hurry the cosmic chef, their relationship would probably have been half-baked! Today, it's just right.

Week 4:

Focus your Mental Energy

Week 4 – PWR® Moves

You're about half-way there! What have you learned about your Self so far? How does your body feel? This week, we're going to continue stepping up our Re-Fuel area. Also, as you learn more on how to focus your mental energy, we're going to Program your Productivity.

1. **REFLECT.** Continue to reflect for at least *15 minutes a day.*

2. **FOCUS.** Continue tuning your mind with positive affirmations every day, at least three times a day. Make sure to Program your Productivity on page 124.

3. **RE-FUEL.** More on the basics:

   a. **Sweat.** Increase your cardiovascular time to at least *25 minutes a day,* for the 6 days of our week.
   b. **Stretch.** Continue stretching for at least *10 minutes a day,* for the 6 days of our week.
   c. **Strengthen.** Increase strengthening to at least *10 minutes a day,* for the 6 days of our week.
   d. **Hydrate.** Continue to make water your drink of choice.
   e. **Eat for Energy.** Continue to add PWR® Foods to your diet and "crowd-out" PWR® Drainers.
   f. **Breathe Deeply.** Continue to practice deep breathing.
   g. **Sleep Soundly.** Continue getting your optimum level and quality of sleep.

4. **CONNECT.** Continue seeking joy every day!

5. **RELEASE.** Every day, continue to let go of *one* bind – a thought, a thing, a commitment, a relationship, a debt, etc.

Give it your best. Log your Progress.

Week 4 - Progress Log

As you receive PWR® Moves each week, rate yourself daily in each area using a 1 – 5 scale (1 =not successful, 5 =very successful).

Action	Day19	Day20	Day21	Day22	Day23	Day24
REFLECT						
Reflect 15 min.						
FOCUS						
Affirmations						
Program Productivity						
RE-FUEL						
Sweat 25 min.						
Stretch 10 min.						
Strengthen 10 min.						
Hydrate 8 glasses						
Add PWR® Foods						
Breathe Deeply						
Sleep Soundly						
CONNECT						
Experience Joy						
RELEASE						
Release 1 Bind						

Accomplishments/Challenges/Notes to Self:

Day 19

Check your Frequency

"That which thought has done, thought can un-do."
- Ernest Holmes

Now that we're about half-way through our 40 days together, it's a perfect opportunity to work on the brain. Many of my clients need a boost in motivation right around this time – which, of course, brings us back to Power Living® Principle #2: **Tune your Mind to the Positive**.

As I shared at the beginning, thought can be used for good – to heal your Self, to direct your life, or for detriment – to hurt, to sabotage. Ask yourself:

- Do I usually expect the best or the worst?
- What mental radio station am I listening to?
- Do I use words like "can't," "but," and "never"?
- Do I beat myself up with negative labels like "stupid"?

You probably don't realize how damaging the little things you say are to your Self and others. Your thoughts, words and attitude affect your consciousness, your health, and, ultimately, your ability to achieve your goals. Negative self-talk, defeating language and a pessimistic attitude generate anxiety and low self-esteem. They block constructive action and positive energy flow.

Recognize and Replace

Recognizing your own thought patterns, and replacing negative ones with positive, is the best strategy for creating an optimistic outlook. Beware of "**The 10 Language Losers"** – language you need to lose if you want to create positive manifestations:

1. **Absolutes** – Ruled by *exaggeration* words or positions: "always," "never," and "everyone." For example: "I always eat too much." "I will never lose weight." Replaced by a more accurate reflection: "I sometimes eat more than I need." "I can lose weight by exercising more."

2. **Shoulds** – Ruled by inherited values: "should," "ought," and "must." For example: "I should be married by now." Replaced by possibilities: "I could meet an amazing man at the party."

3. **No-Can-Do** – Ruled by unbelief and powerlessness. For example, "I can't play that game!" "I can't make it in time." Replaced by possibility thinking and the power of choice: "I'll give it a shot!" "I won't be there this evening, thank you."

4. **The Big But!** – Ruled by a pessimistic "yes, but..." For example: "Yes, but I don't think that will work..." Replaced by an open mind: "Yes, that could work, if..."

5. **All or Nothing** – Ruled by extremes, such as complete failure or total success, and nothing in-between. For example: "Either I lose five pounds by next week, or I quit jogging." Replaced by realistic options: "I want to lose at least two pounds by next week. I will eat healthier and run longer starting today."

6. **Chicken-Little** – Ruled by expectations of the worst. For example, "What if I don't get the job? I'll lose the house!" Replaced by asking questions that presuppose a positive outcome: "How can I prepare for the position? How can I refinance the mortgage?"

7. **Negative Labels** – Ruled by negative phrases which lower self-esteem and belief in your Self and others. For example: "I'm stupid." Replaced by statements about behavior versus identity: "I make poor choices when it comes to my finances."

8. **Stereotyping** – Ruled by preconceived categories for your Self and others. For example: "Overweight people are lazy." Replaced by an open view of people as innately priceless individuals, acknowledging at least *one* thing you find admirable: "I didn't realize you were so adventurous!"

9. **Blamers** – Ruled by assigning guilt to others to avoid responsibility. For example, "Why did you put the dish away like that? No wonder it broke!" Replaced by ways to solve the problem: "Let's reorganize the cabinet so there's more room for the plates."

10. **Complainers** – Ruled by complaining and dwelling on the problem. For example, "I can't believe I didn't get the job! I'm sure the manager sabotaged me!" Replaced with possible solutions and forward-thinking: "How can I learn from this experience so my next interview is better?"

Although our attitudes and thought patterns develop from the time we are children, we *can* change them through conscious, consistent action. Every morning choose to be in a good mood. If something unexpected happens, choose to learn from it instead of being a victim. If you catch negative self-talk, immediately replace it with a realistic, positive thought.

> "We don't see things as they are. We see them as we are."
> - Anais Nis

Have your affirmations, power words and "breath prayers" handy. Choose to project an optimistic view, and see how grace miraculously responds.

A positive outlook can turn your life around, causing a chain reaction of favorable thoughts, events, and outcomes. Tune your mind to a station you *want* to listen to and enjoy!

Reality Check

Today we're focused on **thoughts, language and attitude**. Monitor your thoughts for a day. Be a witness to your inner chatter and write it down at random times.

Thoughts/Overall Attitude

____

____

____

Major Themes. For example, do you beat your Self up on how you look, or your work performance?

____

____

____

% Negative Thoughts: _____ **% Positive Thoughts:** _____

Most Common Critical Thoughts

1. ____

2. ____

3. ____

Remember to sweat for at least 25 minutes today.

Fine-tune your Focus

"Often he who does too much does too little."
- Italian Proverb

Wow! The mind is amazing, isn't it? Think about this: whatever you focus on manifests as reality in your life. It's been put another way: whatever you are intimate with, you will birth. Are you pregnant with possibilities or catastrophes?

You can focus on reaching your goals through *concentration* or on the obstacles that stand in your way by *worrying*. It's your choice! Ask yourself:

- Is my attention scattered?
- Am I in a constant reactive state?
- How often do I achieve sustained focus on a task?
- Am I busy all the time and *still* fail to get things done?

The key is to use the power of the mind by consciously directing your attention to desired outcomes.

The Myth of Multitasking

In a society that values "multitasking," it is challenging to maintain focus. We often get rewarded for polyphasic behavior - doing several things simultaneously – because it *seems* more productive. Yet, when you try to do everything at once, you dilute your efforts and compromise the results.

When I was at MTV, I was the queen of multitasking. Even though my assistant was extremely efficient, I still saw the need to talk on the phone, type on the computer, watch TV, and listen to a CD - all at the same time. I finally realized that I wasn't working smart. Eventually, I learned that by really focusing on *one* thing at a time, I was able to be more creative and get the job done quicker. I'm not down on multitasking altogether! It can be efficient when both tasks don't require your full creative energy, such as:

- Commuting on a train and reading a book.
- Driving and listening to a motivational tape.
- Running on the treadmill and watching the news.

The Power of Meditation

Learning how to meditate can help you harness your energy and increase your ability to focus. Meditation allows you to take a break from the incessant stream of thoughts flowing through your mind. Once again, it is about *being* rather than *doing*. It's a practical way to investigate your inner nature through a process of self-observation, self-inquiry and mindful action.

Although it can be a spiritual practice, meditation is not about a specific religion. Instead it is a method of living consciously in the moment without judgment, allowing you to receive guidance from your own Higher Power.

> "And in His law
> he meditates
> day and night."
> - Psalms 1:2

Meditation has been found to reduce stress, and benefit sleep disorders, headaches, depression, and high blood pressure. Rather than withdrawing from the world, clearing the mind can help you enjoy life more fully - gaining greater clarity, peace and Purpose. There are a variety of techniques. For example, you can focus on your breath, a candle, a word or phrase, a picture or sound. Practice different techniques to find one that works for you. Make a point to set aside a certain time for stillness and silence each day.

Reality Check

Today we're dealing with **focus.** Monitor your work habits for a day. Be a witness to your process and write down notes on what you observe.

How was my energy? Was it scattered or focused? Explain.

____

____

____

Most Common Distractions

1. ______________________________

2. ______________________________

3. ______________________________

Practice one of the meditation techniques. Note your comments on the process or thoughts that surfaced during or after.

____

____

____

Remember to drink at least 8 glasses of purified water today.

Boost your Brain Power

"Old age is like everything else.
To make a success of it, you've got to start young."
- Fred Astaire

The brain, with its astounding computational power, is the main server of our system. Are you doing things to decrease its operating potential or boost its functioning ability? Ask yourself:

- How often do I have "brain fog"?
- Can I readily remember names and numbers?
- Do I ever walk in a room and *instantly* forget what I went in there for?

Sometimes you may feel like you're losing your mind, and that could be true. There are many reasons why we forget things. Often the mind is simply just too busy. Brain drain can also come from sickness, lack of exercise and sleep, eating highly processed sugary foods, a depressed emotional state, alcohol, tobacco, and certain drugs. All of these factors can affect how well you make memories and can interfere with recall.

Keep the Wires Alive

Recent studies have shown that stress plays a role in accelerating brain aging. Of course, my ears perk up when I hear reports like that since I endured so many years of unreleased stress which eventually landed me in the hospital. Although I've healed my body, I often wonder whether I've sustained damage to my brain cells. Needless to say, I am *very* interested in ways to boost brain power! The good news is there are ways to optimize the brain's functioning power and lengthen your mentally active years. Let me share with you my "**Top 5 Brain Boosters**:"

1. **Control stress.** Stress is a part of life; the key is how you manage it. Use techniques to relax and focus, such as deep breathing, meditation, affirmation and visualization. Writing in a journal will help you emotionally and mentally. Stay away from environmental stress from pesticides and solvents.

2. **Eat Smart.** Choose items on the PWR® Foods list. Protein, whole grains and the Omega-3 fatty acids are particularly important. Limit dairy products and stay away from the PWR® Drainers. Take a multivitamin that gives you the B-complex, iron, E, C, A, zinc, calcium, selenium and coenzyme Q-10. Certain herbs may be helpful such as ginseng and astragalus. Garlic and turmeric are also great. Always check with your doctor before adding natural herbal treatments to make sure they do not interfere with prescribed medicines.

3. **Exercise.** Keep the blood flowing to the brain. Cardiovascular exercise will boost short-term memory and help control blood pressure, atherosclerosis, high cholesterol and diabetes – all risk factors for cerebrovascular compromise.

4. **Seek Cognitive Challenges**. Do mental aerobics with problem-solving, mystery books, puzzles and word games. Get involved in activities that keep you mentally on the move, such as community groups and continuing education classes.

5. **Use Mind Tricks.** When trying to remember a name, take a mental snapshot and use a rhyme or association. Engage *all* of your senses. Group digits, like 857-234-5896. Use mnemonics. For example, "Every good boy does fine" in music, representing E-G-B-D-F, the notes of the treble staff. Talk out loud to your Self while doing a task you want to remember.

Reality Check

Today we're focused on **brain power**.

How would I describe my memory power? Do you forget things regularly? Is your mind often cloudy?

___

___

___

What foods/herbs will I add to boost my brain power?

___

___

What foods/habits will I "crowd-out" to boost my brain power?

___

___

What are 3 ways I can challenge my mind?

1. ___

2. ___

3. ___

Remember to practice deep breathing today.

Day 22

Cultivate Intuition

"The soul of God is poured into the world
through the thoughts of men."
- Ralph Waldo Emerson

Intuition plays a filtering role in the decisions you make every day – from which route to take, to whom to trust. For example, having a "bad feeling" about a person may save you from a disastrous business deal; or having a "sudden thought" to go down a certain street could lead to a real estate find. Ask yourself:

- How often do I follow my gut instinct?
- Do I listen more to others than my own intuition?
- Have I ever ignored a "hunch" and then regretted it later?

Psychologist Carl Jung describes intuition as "a basic psychological function that explores the unknown and senses possibilities and implications which may not be readily apparent." It provides an additional level of information that does not come from the logical side of the brain.

If you are spiritual, intuition can be seen as guidance from your Higher Power. It can take on many forms: images, words in your mind, vivid dreams, emotions, or a sense of direct knowing.

"A moment's insight
is sometimes worth
a life's experience."
- Oliver Wendell Holmes

Everyone is gifted with intuition. Some people trust it and life seems to flow. Others are ruled by fear, which undermines the intuitive voice blocking potential opportunities. Being more in touch with your intuition -- tuning into it, recognizing its truth, and acting upon it - can help you make wiser decisions, resolve problems more quickly, and experience life to its fullest.

Tap into your Dreams

I receive many of my own inspirations in dreams. Some musicians say that songs come to them in that way. Friedrich Kekule, the German chemist, discovered the structure of benzene in a dream. Research has confirmed that the average person dreams between 90 to 120 minutes every night, 3 to 7 times a night. Some of us remember several dreams nightly, while others have no recall at all. Interference of dreams can come from drugs, alcohol, caffeine, serious depression – or simply not getting enough REM sleep.

Dreams can play an important role in your spiritual journey. By giving your Self pre-sleep suggestions, through a process called *dream incubation,* you can solve problems while you sleep allowing the divine tutor to step in and help.

> "Let us learn to dream, and then we may perhaps find the truth."
> - Friedrich Kekule

You may also experience *lucid dreaming,* in which you are aware you are dreaming while still asleep. The increased clarity and directable nature of the lucid state often enables you to wake with clear creative insights and inspiration. As far back as recorded history, dreams have been employed for guidance and healing. Tap into the power of your own dreams. If you pay attention, you may come face-to-face with the deepest truths about your unconscious thoughts and feelings.

Reality Check

Today we're focused on **intuition and dreams**. Tune into your "hunches" for a day. Act on them. See if the day flows in a different way than the day before.

How did intuition play a role in my day?

Dream Themes. Tell your Self that you want to remember your dreams. Keep a journal, penlight and pen next to your bed. When you wake up, try to move as little as possible. Write down all of your dreams. Notice the main aspects and themes.

Remember to stretch for at least 10 minutes today.

Program your Productivity

"It's not the load that breaks you down,
it's the way you carry it."
- Lena Horne

Work is not laborious if you're in the flow. It goes back to self-awareness and self-control. Ask yourself:

- Do I know my own body's rhythm?
- Do I manage my time and energy effectively?
- Am I alert when I need to be, such as in a meeting or writing a proposal?

Once you learn how to control your energy you will live in a way so that you have maximum power when you need it. *Full in...* instead of *spread thin!* It's like an athlete training for the Olympics, but the game is life.

Prime Work - Peak Energy

To be most productive and in synch with your body's natural rhythm, follow one primary rule:

Schedule prime mental work during peak "think" time.

The body has its own timekeeper – the circadian rhythm, a 24-hour cycle which corresponds to the cycles of light and darkness. Heart rate, body temperature, hormone levels, and alertness change in accordance to the time of day. There is no single time of peak performance, but rather different peak times for different types of tasks. **The Power Living® Productivity Planner** can help you schedule your day most effectively:

Power Living® Productivity Planner		
Zone	**Time**	**Type of Work**
1	**6am – 9am**	**Creative/Strategic** Good time for meditating and receiving inspirations, as well as writing and creative brainstorming.
2	**9am – 12pm**	**Logical/Strategic** Prime time for organizing, planning, creative thinking, writing, editing. Reasoning skills are high, as well as short-term memory. Complex decision-making skills are at their peak between 11am - 12pm.
3	**12pm – 3pm**	**Communication** Good time for making connections. Cheeriness is high. Mental alertness declines. Daydreaming increases. Between 2-3pm the body temperature drops and sleepiness is likely to kick in.
4	**3pm – 6pm**	**Administrative/Routine** Performance is high for repetitive tasks requiring motor activity, such as sorting mail and filing. Alertness returns around 4pm. Long-term memory is high and reaction time is swift. Good time to work on small projects.
5	**6pm – 10pm**	**Active/Creative** Alertness continues. A good creative time for many. Prime time to exercise and play as well.
6	**10pm – 6am**	**Sleep Time** Time for rest and repair.

You can extend your peak energy times for various tasks using food and recovery strategies. A lot of the coaching work I do with executives and entrepreneurs is focused on customizing these strategies for their particular work environments.

What if you work the late shift? Whether you are an emergency room doctor or a jazz musician, you may not work 9-to-5. According to various studies, those who work in a *rotating* shift will not really adapt to the changes. However, people who work on a *permanent* night shift will find that their body rhythms adjust. In both cases, there *are* strategies to maximize energy.

Take a Mini-Escape

No matter what your profession, studies have shown that it is important to take a break every 90 to 120 minutes for peak performance. Even if you simply take a walk around the block – get up and change your environment.

When I was a corporate executive, I used to work for hours straight-through and wonder why my attention was wandering. Sometimes I would even eat lunch *and* dinner at my desk. I wasn't using my mind and energy efficiently. No wonder I was at work so late!

> "Every now and then go away, have a little relaxation, for when you come back to your judgment will be surer."
> - Leonardo da Vinci

Many of my clients use the *Power Living®: Mini-Escapes* relaxation CD during their workday. From breath awareness and visualization to meditation and affirmations, it offers 70 minutes of 3-to-12-minute instant relaxation breaks.

Another version of a mini-escape is to do a "News Fast." You typically do a fast to purify your body. It's also good to detoxify the mind every once and awhile. Choose at least one day a week to ease up on your media consumption. Don't watch the news, turn off the radio, and restrain yourself from wandering online. Don't worry… the world won't end – and if it does, you will certainly hear about it from your neighbors! If your job requires you to watch the media like mine did, limit your time to just the headlines. Your entire psyche will thank you.

Reality Check

Today we're focused on **productivity**. Create a master schedule that works best for your type of tasks. Although it may vary slightly from day-to-day, think about your overall energy flow.

Power Living® Productivity Planner		
Zone	**Time**	**Type of Work**
1	**6am – 9am**	**Creative/Strategic**
2	**9am – 12pm**	**Logical/Strategic**
3	**12pm – 3pm**	**Communication**
4	**3pm – 6pm**	**Administrative/Routine**
5	**6pm – 10pm**	**Active/Creative**
6	**10pm – 6am**	**Sleep Time**

Remember to experience joy today.

Day 24

Make Clear Commitments

"The moment one definitely commits oneself,
then providence moves too. All sorts of things occur
to help one that would never otherwise have occurred."
- Johann Wolfgang von Goethe

Now that you know what type of work to do when, make a pledge to actually stick to it. Ask yourself:

- What am I committed to?
- Do my actions represent that commitment?
- Do my commitments support my life vision?
- Do others respect my boundaries?

A commitment is a specific promise, which is followed through over time – such as eliminating sugar from your diet this month, or becoming self-employed by next year. Being able to make a commitment, and keep it, is one of the key indicators to success.

Make Values-Driven Decisions

Remember those core values from Week 3? This is where they become very important. Let your values guide your decisions. Make commitments that are in synch with your Purpose.

> "I know the price of success: dedication, hard work, and an unremitting devotation to things you want to see happen."
> - Frank Lloyd Wright

Distinguish between short-term targets, such as losing 10 pounds, and lifelong commitments, such as raising loving kids. Eliminate activities that don't fit your grand plan. Living your values actually makes it easier to say "No" to things without guilt.

In a society that promotes convenience and instant gratification, it's easy to be distracted from your goals. Commitment requires self-discipline, perseverance, and sacrifice. It often doesn't allow you to "keep your options open." Therefore, you may fear commitment because of the uncertainly of the outcome. Understand that the commitments you make shape your identity and affect your destiny. By being clear and specific in your choices, you're exercising personal power and allowing providence to work for you.

Teach People How to Treat You

> "Simply let your 'Yes' be 'Yes,' and your 'No,' 'No.'"
> - Matthew 5:37

Once you've set the schedule that works best for your energy, teach people how to treat you. For example:

- If you say you're going to write from 8am to 10am and don't want to be disturbed... then turn off the phone.
- If you say you're *not* going to work from home... then don't answer office email at 10pm.
- If you say you want the family to start eating healthier... then don't buy the sugar-laden cereal next time your child or spouse asks for it.

Set clear boundaries and live by your word – whether it's a promise to your Self or to another. When you let others know your priorities and take control of your own life, you experience inner peace and immense satisfaction. Remember, the power of commitment grows day-by-day. Don't fall prey to procrastination or rationalization. Do what *you* have to do NOW!

Reality Check

Today we're focused on **commitment**.

What commitments have I made to my Self?

What commitments can I eliminate that don't fit my vision?

How can I better teach people how to treat me?

Remember to strengthen for at least 10 minutes today.

A PWR® Moment

Channeling Creativity

The Power of Honoring Inspiration

My Dad was 100% authentic, 100% of the time... a little eccentric, always original. That was his greatest gift to the world. "No double-layered human being here" as he wrote in *Africa is a Woman*. He let his light shine.

He always spoke his mind. If he had something to say, he would tell you directly to your face. He's the only person I know who - when a dog barked at him, he would bark back... and scare the dog! He kept us on our toes. Sometimes, we didn't know what he was going to do in a given moment. Other times he was very predictable in his encouragement and love.

As a writer, producer and composer, he epitomized pure creativity - always with a pen and paper in hand in case a thought, song, or poem came to mind. He honored his inspirations by *instantly* writing them down. He wrote countless songs and plays and, together with Mom, produced over 100 theatrical performances around the world. Although he was covered by the media through the years and taught many famous students - from tennis great Althea Gibson to movie-star Denzel Washington, he was not thinking about the money his work would generate - he was simply being a divine conduit. He was living from his Core, inspiring many along the way. Knowing that Dad's spirit would continue to create, my brother included a pen and pad in his casket, *just in case* Dad had some truly divine inspirations!

Week 5:

Engage your Emotional Energy

Week 5 – PWR® Moves

Welcome to Week 5! Did last week start getting your mind in order? This week, we're going to continue stepping up our Re-Fuel area. Also, as you learn how to engage your emotional energy, we're going to add more reflection time.

1. **REFLECT.** Increase your reflection time to at least *20 minutes a day* – adding 5 minutes to your evening time.

2. **FOCUS.** Continue tuning your mind with positive affirmations every day, at least three times a day. Continue to program your productivity for peak performance.

3. **RE-FUEL.** More on the basics:

   a. **Sweat.** Increase your cardiovascular time to at least *30 minutes a day,* for the 6 days of our week.
   b. **Stretch.** Continue stretching for at least *15 minutes a day,* for the 6 days of our week.
   c. **Strengthen.** Increase strengthening for at least *15 minutes a day,* for the 6 days of our week.
   d. **Hydrate.** Continue to make water your drink of choice.
   e. **Eat for Energy.** Continue to add PWR® Foods to your diet and "crowd-out" PWR® Drainers.
   f. **Breathe Deeply.** Continue to practice deep breathing.
   g. **Sleep Soundly.** Continue getting your optimum level and quality of sleep.

4. **CONNECT.** Continue seeking joy every day.

5. **RELEASE.** Every day, continue to let go of *one* bind – a thought, a thing, a commitment, a relationship, a debt, etc.

Give it your best. Log your Progress.

Week 5 - Progress Log

As you receive PWR® Moves each week, rate yourself daily in each area using a 1 – 5 scale (1 =not successful, 5 =very successful).

Action	Day25	Day26	Day27	Day28	Day29	Day30
REFLECT						
Reflect 20 min.						
FOCUS						
Affirmations						
Program Productivity						
RE-FUEL						
Sweat 30 min.						
Stretch 15 min.						
Strengthen 15 min.						
Hydrate 8 glasses						
Add PWR® Foods						
Breathe Deeply						
Sleep Soundly						
CONNECT						
Experience Joy						
RELEASE						
Release 1 Bind						

Accomplishments/Challenges/Notes to Self:

Embrace Change

"The important thing is this: to be able at any moment to sacrifice what we are for what we could become."
- Charles DuBois

Given everything you've learned so far in our Practice, you may realize that there are some things in your life that need to change. This is where Power Living® Principle #4: **Be a Humble Warrior** really becomes important. Ask yourself:

- How peaceful am I through a transition?
- Do I embrace change or run away from it?
- When was the last time I prompted a major shift in my behavior without it being initiated by a crisis?

As Heraclitus said, "There is nothing permanent except change." Change is inevitable. It is a part of life. The only way to grow is to constantly renew and rejuvenate ourselves, just as our cells renew in our bodies. Life is based on *circulation* and *flow*.

The Fours Stages of Change

If you understand the process of change, you can ride with it. The Wheel of Life is an ancient model describing the emotions of change. I have updated the representation in "**The Four Stages of Change**," using my own nature-inspired metaphor.

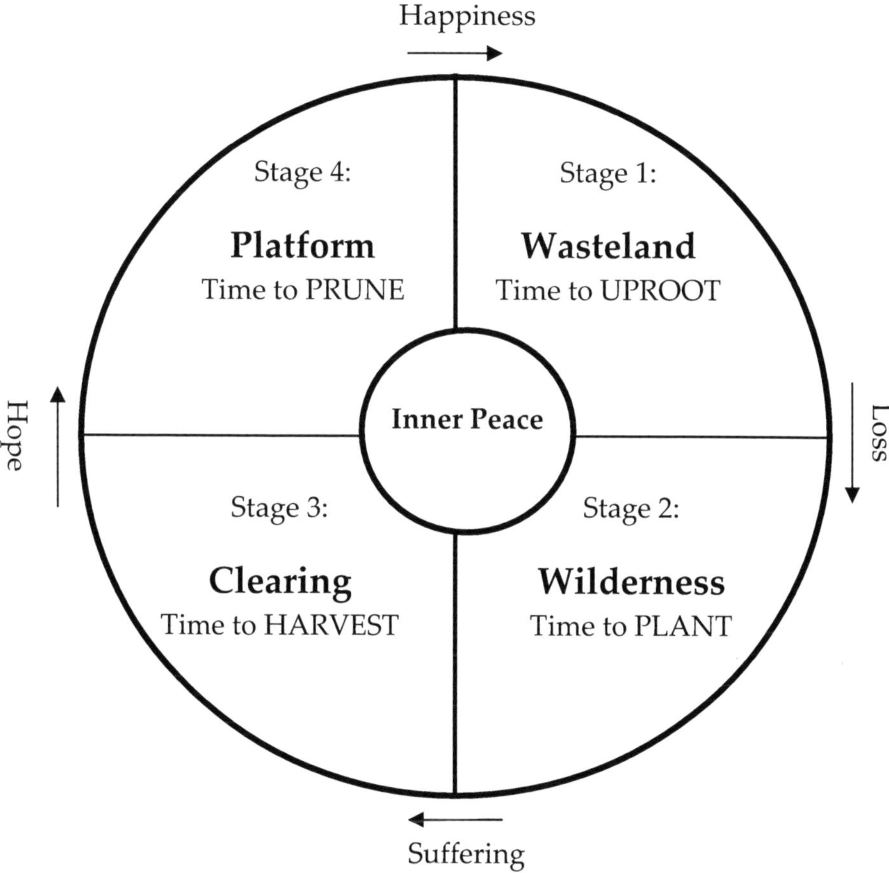

The wheel's lesson is that there are only four positions in life: happiness, loss, suffering and hope. Change always comes. We can't circumvent the stages. Because the wheel always turns, this is a constant process. Going through these stages is the only way to grow. The one thing that does not move is the center of the wheel – the axis, which I call the Core. This is your inner peace coming from faith, love and joy. This carries you through each round. If you are tapped into your Core, you will remain peaceful through each cycle of change.

With each change, certain action is required:

1. **Wasteland** – The stage of Loss when a change is happening. It's time to assess the situation and Uproot... recognize and begin to replace PWR®-draining habits
2. **Wilderness** – The stage of Suffering - which really means "to allow, to experience" - when you must work through the change. It is the transition period. It's time to Plant... plan and create an environment for success.
3. **Clearing** – The stage of Hope where you see a light at the end of the tunnel. It's time to Harvest... take consistent action following your new plan.
4. **Platform** – The stage of Happiness where you reach a new level of normalcy. It's time to Prune... make adjustments, deal with lapses and prevent relapses, understanding that happiness is fleeting and you will ride the wheel again!

Crisis is a Dangerous Opportunity

Many people fear change because it always involves some type of loss, even if it is a positive change like marriage - which brings loss of your old identity. People also don't want to suffer. However, it is out of *experiencing* that hope arises and you can return to a new state of equilibrium. As you spiral through more evolved states, you grow psychologically and spiritually. This is why change is good. It allows you to live more fully.

The Chinese word for crisis is similar to the faces of change. It is composed of two separate characters. One means danger and the other means opportunity. The proper translation is, "Crisis is a dangerous opportunity." If you want to create a successful life, you must embrace change. Use it as a catalyst for growth. When any change occurs – whether it comes from an outside source or an internal decision – remain flexible and open your Self to see the opportunity. Remember... in movement there is life and in change there is power!

Reality Check

Today we're focused on **change**. Think of a major change you want to – or have to – make, or are already making.

How will I approach this change?

In what stage am I currently with this particular change?

Understanding the stages of change, what action must I take?

Remember to sweat for at least 30 minutes today.

Count It All Joy

"God brings men into deep waters not to drown them, but to cleanse them."
- James H. Aughey

The Bible says in James 1:2, "My brethren, count it all joy whenever you face trials of many kinds, because you know that the testing of your faith develops perseverance. Perseverance must finish its work so that you may be mature and complete, not lacking anything." Do you really count it *all* joy? Ask yourself:

- How often do I acknowledge my blessings?
- Do I expect more from the Universe when I don't appreciate what I already have?
- When something seemingly bad happens, do I see the good in it?

The surest path to success is through the fire. By shifting your perspective on adversity, viewing it as part of your refinement process, you'll learn to embrace change and jump into the fire. As I've said before, making this journey depends on the strength of your Core and the faith in your path.

Joy Connects Us to Our Core

As you've seen from "The Four Stages of Change," inner peace comes from cultivating faith, love and joy. We've already talked about the importance of growing in faith. Remember, every time you *try your faith*, you build character, and faith becomes a more powerful element in your life. Love is another guiding force, which we'll discuss tomorrow. Right now let's focus on joy.

What is the difference between joy and happiness? Happiness is related to the word "hap," which implies happenstance – a state that is fleeting and based on luck versus effort. In our culture, happiness is often derived from material things and external rewards. Joy is a much deeper and intense experience. It's about *connection* – with your Self, with others, and the Universe. It is being able to appreciate your special place in this world, understanding that it's really about inspiring versus acquiring.

Gratitude as a Way of Life

To experience the depth of joy it is important to make gratitude a way of life. The more you are grateful for, the more will be given to you and the more you can give to others. Thankfulness is the most powerful statement to your Creator; an affirmation that even before you ask, the answer is there. Every morning, you've been given the gift of another day. Use *at least one* of the 86,400 seconds to say, "thank you."

Be thankful even for difficult times. From cash flow shortages to relationship challenges, every problem is an opportunity to be refined. One way to express your gratitude is to do something for others. By paying "in kind," you are investing your talents in another's good.

> "I had the blues because I had no shoes until upon the street I met a man who had no feet."
> - Denis Waitely

Remember that your personal net worth is not determined by the size of your checking account balance. Show appreciation for the river of abundance that flows through your life each and every day. When you do a mental and spiritual inventory of all that you have, you will realize that you are very rich indeed.

<u>Reality Check</u>

Today we're focused on **<u>joy and gratitude</u>**.

<u>What brings me joy?</u>

____

____

<u>What am I thankful for right now?</u> Make a gratitude list. It could start off with simply being alive!

1. ______________________________________
2. ______________________________________
3. ______________________________________
4. ______________________________________
5. ______________________________________
6. ______________________________________
7. ______________________________________
8. ______________________________________
9. ______________________________________
10. ______________________________________

Remember to release one bind today.

Lead with Love

"Love possesses not nor would it be possessed;
for love is sufficient unto love."
- Kahlil Gibran

Love is the other quality that allows us to remain peaceful through change. It is a major source of energy. Ask yourself:

- Do I love unconditionally?
- Am I open to real intimacy?
- Do my words and actions express a spirit of caring?

We are all born with an innate desire to be loved and accepted. Without love, life can feel empty and meaningless. However, love -- from a mother, a partner, a friend -- can build self-esteem and be the boost that propels you to happiness and achievement. Words of encouragement, even from a stranger, can save a life.

Choose To Love

The Ancient Greeks named four types of love: 1) *Philios,* friendship love; 2) *Eros,* physical love; 3) *Storge,* maternal love; and 4) *Agape,* unconditional love. The Bible's "love chapter," 1 Corinthians 13, gives us a summary of "agape" love. It is patient, kind, not jealous, boastful or rude. It bears, believes, hopes and endures all things. Love never fails.

Choose to approach each day with unselfish caring, showing concern for the welfare of others. Treasure the love you receive, and the love that emanates from Nature and the Universe. Love for the satisfaction of giving rather than receiving. Give the gift of focused attention to those you love. Material presents are nice, but your Presence is the greatest gift of all. Share love freely, willingly and without expectation, and your life will be full of joy.

Allow Intimacy In

Humans are social beings. One of our deepest needs is to feel connected – to others and the Universe as a whole. We do not want to be alone. Ironically, our high tech society, with disposable emails and individual iPods, has actually driven us away from true intimacy – which is the key to lasting relationships, psychological healing, spiritual growth and even good health.

Intimacy is not just a physical act, but is a full emotional union between two people. It requires honesty, direct communication, maturity and trust. Through a process of mutual self-disclosure, each person must open up to one another's differences.

> "Passion is the quickest to develop, and the quickest to fade. Intimacy develops more slowly and commitment more gradually still."
> - Robert Steinberg

Many people fear intimacy because it requires them to be vulnerable and let go of being "perfect." This fear actually drives them to remain in control (or at least *appear* that way!), blocking the blessing of ultimate expression and togetherness. When you let another person enter your world, life actually becomes easier. Disclosing your Self to another allows you to be loved for who you truly are. The other person can help you identify "blind" spots and challenge you to face your fears, becoming a companion on your spiritual journey. Starting today, prepare your Self for intimacy. Remove your mask. Open your heart up to the possibilities of a deep personal partnership. It will give you the freedom and support to remain Present and authentic, allowing you to love more passionately and experience life more fully.

Reality Check

Today we're focused on **love and intimacy**.

How can I develop more intimacy in my relationships?

____

____

Acts of Kindness. Make a list of ways to share love with others. It could start off with smiling at one person today!

1. ____
2. ____
3. ____
4. ____
5. ____
6. ____
7. ____
8. ____
9. ____
10. ____

Remember to practice deep breathing today.

Listen to Connect

"Let the wise listen and add to their learning,
and let the discerning get guidance."
- Proverbs 1:5

Listening effectively is a powerful life skill. It can lead to more fulfilling personal and professional relationships, improved business performance, and a strong knowledge base. When you listen to your Self, you can also gain greater awareness, self-esteem, and clarity of vision. Ask yourself:

- How well do I listen?
- What does it feel like when someone really listens to me?
- Do I formulate my response before the other person is even finished speaking?

Research shows that at least 40 percent of our waking hours are spent listening. However, within a few minutes following a discussion, the average listener is able to recall only 25 percent or less of what he or she heard.

Pay Attention

We all have a yearning to be understood. Most people jockey for a position to talk, or tune out, instead of paying attention during a conversation. Listening is more than just hearing and waiting for your turn to speak. It is an *active* process that requires energy, discipline and mindfulness.

You may have to agree to take turns listening. For example: "I will listen to you and pay attention, if you will give me a chance to do the same thing later on." Either way, the essence of good listening is having empathy, and an attitude of respect and encouragement. It involves suspension of judgment -- making the other person feel important, confident and safe. And please note that listening is not always tied to giving advice!

Both of my parents are communications experts. My Mom is a journalist and my Dad, as early as the 1950s, was known as Mr. Speech. Here are some basic rules from the "Kennedy School of Thought." I call them "**The 3 Steps to Listening Success**:"

1. **Stop talking.** When you talk, you repeat what you already know; when you listen, you often learn something.
2. **Listen to the *whole* message.** Observe both the verbal and non-verbal communication. Note what is *not* said.
3. **Be fully Present.** Maintain eye contact, paraphrase and ask questions for clarity. Be conscious of your tone. Have empathy, creating a safe environment for sharing.

Extend Forgiveness

To be a humble warrior, you must learn how to forgive. Forgiveness is not an emotion, it's a choice. To withhold forgiveness is to choose to continue to be a victim – since holding a grudge hurts *you* more than the other person. It consumes your energy and clouds your vision.

> "For every minute you are angry, you lose sixty seconds of happiness."
> - Emerson

Forgiving someone does not necessarily condone their action; it simply releases it to the Universe. As Romans 8:33-34 says, "It is God who justifies? Who is he that condemns?" Extend forgiveness to someone who has hurt you and you will receive the gift of inner peace.

Reality Check

Today we're focused on **listening and forgiveness**.

Listening Log. Monitor your interactions today to see how well you listen. Note your observations.

____

____

____

____

Forgive Your Self. What do you need to forgive your Self for?

____

____

____

____

Forgive Others. Who do you need to forgive? When will you?

____

____

____

Remember to eat some PWR® Foods today.

Nurture your Self

"You, yourself, as much as anybody in the entire universe, deserve your love and affection."
- Buddha

It is not possible to give fully to others and experience joy, if you don't love your Self. Answer the following:

- Do I often have feelings of falling short?
- Do I accept my Self right in this moment?
- Do I give to others and ignore my own needs?

Lack of self-acceptance causes you to be dependent on other people and things to make you feel good about your Self. You are more likely to suffer from low self-esteem, feel misunderstood, experience failed relationships, and exhibit addictive behavior. You may use "if-then" clauses in establishing conditions for loving your Self: "*If* I lose 10 pounds, *then* I'll be worthy."

Tame the Inner Critic

We've learned how important thoughts, words and attitude are in managing our mental energy. Self-acceptance is the key to our emotional well-being as well. It is an agreement with your Self to appreciate, respect, accept and support who you are *right now,* even those parts you would like to eventually change. It is honoring your unique Purpose, without putting preset limits on what you can achieve.

Acceptance does not mean complacency. Instead, it means that you are Present and have stopped resisting what your experience is now. See yourself for who you are – both your strengths and your weaknesses.

> "A man cannot be comfortable without his own self-approval."
> - Mark Twain

Strive to be the best you can, but accept that you are human and may make mistakes. Recognize that self-acceptance happens over time. When you accept your Core Self unconditionally, you will be open to receive life, resulting in a sense of clarity, increased effectiveness, and a feeling of peace and progress.

Love Your Self First

It is more important to like yourself, than for others to like you. Self-love is the first step toward success and happiness in life. If you don't love your Self, you will always feel that you do not deserve opportunities, fulfilling relationships and prosperity. You may experience self-sabotage and self-abuse – which opens the window for exploitation from others. You are more likely to become involved in a codependent relationship. You might feel lonely even when you are with your partner.

True self-love is not the same as narcissism. A person, who goes out of his way to show his importance, is actually covering up low self-esteem. When you feel a sense of inner acceptance, there is no need to prove anything to others. It is easier to take rejection in stride because you know that it is not about you. You accept your worth as a divine birthright.

Become your own best friend. Spend time noticing who you are. See the "alone" hours as a gift rather than a curse. Indulge your Self each day. Sit in the park. See the movie *you* want to see. Take a hot bath. When you love your Self, you exude an energy that attracts what and who you need into your world.

Reality Check

Today we're focused on **self-love**.

Love Note. Write a love note to your Self.

How can I nurture my Self? You could start with a bubble bath!

1.
2.
3.
4.
5.
6.
7.
8.
9.
10.

Remember to drink at least 8 glasses of purified water today.

Pause & Play

"In every real [wo]man
a child is hidden that wants to play."
- Friedrich Nietzsche

One way to nurture your spirit is to simply play! We've already learned that it's important to take a break every 90 to 120 minutes for peak mental performance. It's also important to pause and play for your emotional well-being. Ask yourself:

- How many times a day do I laugh?
- Do I often respond spontaneously to things?
- How playful am I in my personal relationships?

Life should be a balance between effort and ease. Oftentimes people operate at the extremes – constantly in motion, or afraid to take action. Instead, aim to achieve a state of equilibrium.

Play Every Day

People who know how to play and have fun are often more relaxed and capable of handling stressful situations. Play is one of the most effective ways to manage and release the buildup of daily tension. It also taps into the right hemisphere of the brain that spurs imagination, creativity and intuition.

Take your pet for a walk or begin a craft. Try to look at the world through a child's eyes. Marvel at the wonders around you. Be with children and frolic with them, or simply observe their enjoyment. See their complete lack of inhibition and self-criticism.

Then find a "buddy"– someone to have fun with. It could be someone right in front of you, such as a colleague at work.

External rewards – money, recognition, and respect – pale in comparison to the emotional and spiritual benefits you receive from playing. Play can make your larger upsets seem smaller, expand your limited picture, and get you to see more than your problems or pressures.

Laugh Often

It has been reported that a child laughs 400 times a day on average, while an adult laughs only 15 times a day. Adults need to lighten up and reap the healing benefits of laughter.

> "A merry heart doeth good like a medicine, but a broken spirit drieth the bones."
> - Proverbs 17:22

Laughter has been called God's holy medicine. An instinctive behavior, laughter stimulates the circulation, energizes the lungs, lowers blood pressure, alleviates depression, and releases endorphins, which can help control pain. It is often called "internal aerobics" because it improves muscle tone. Researchers calculate that 100 laughs equal about 10 minutes on a rowing machine, or 15 minutes on an exercise bike.

Humor can be an empowerment tool. When you laugh at setbacks you take a more relaxed attitude, and no longer feel sorry for your Self. You feel more in control. You can also use humor to break tension and ease communication in personal and business relationships. Above all, the spirit of laughter reminds you to live fully in the Present.

Create a collection of your best laughter sources, such as newspaper comics, funny movies, and television bloopers. Share jokes with friends and family. Give others a chuckle. If you want to increase your enjoyment of life, laugh often and heartily.

Reality Check

Today we're focused on **play and laughter**.

Mood-Changers. Note instant mood-changers. It could be a particular song, a picture, an activity, a joke, or a friend.

____

____

Play List. What will you do for fun - alone or with other people?

1. ____

2. ____

3. ____

4. ____

5. ____

6. ____

7. ____

8. ____

9. ____

10. ____

Remember to strengthen for at least 15 minutes today.

A PWR® Moment

The Trial of the Century

The Power of Perseverance

I once read that the human body is designed for a maximum life span of about 120 years. When I was lying in the hospital with various tubes hooked up to me while I was still in my twenties, I remembered that statistic. It made me a little upset with God. I felt cheated. I had been a good person all of my life. Yes, I was a bit neurotic about work, but I had not seriously wronged anyone and I loved my family deeply – even though I hadn't recently spent much time with them. I was wondering why this horrible experience was happening to me. My goal was to hit the century mark like my great Aunt Jane, but my odds looked grim.

Now, I understand that I was being prepared for something even greater – my Purpose. I've learned that with trials come triumphs. Generally, when you pass a test you move on to the next level. It takes perseverance to endure. I had many tests along the way. Those 10 days in the hospital were just the start. Over the next seven years, I crafted a new being. It took me one year to leave my small apartment. Two years to leave my job. Three years to leave my relationship. Four years to heal again. Five years to find my Purpose. Six years to start my business. Seven years to *begin* to see results and live anew. I now know that my true work is the constant process of discovery, preparing yet again for the next trial… leading me to the trial of the century in the most Supreme of all courts!

Week 6:

Detoxify your Environmental Energy

Week 6 – PWR® Moves

Welcome to Week 6! We're moving down the home stretch now. Did you experience more joy last week? This week, we've hit our goals for the Re-Fuel area so simply maintain what you've started. Also, as you learn more on how to detoxify your environmental energy, we're going to add some playtime.

1. **REFLECT.** Continue to reflect for at least *20 minutes a day.*

2. **FOCUS.** Continue tuning your mind with positive affirmations every day, at least three times a day. Continue to program your productivity for peak performance.

3. **RE-FUEL.** Continue the basics:

   a. **Sweat.** Continue cardiovascular for at least *30 minutes a day*, for the 6 days of our week.
   b. **Stretch.** Continue stretching for at least *15 minutes a day*, for the 6 days of our week.
   c. **Strengthen.** Continue strengthening for at least *15 minutes a day*, for the 6 days of our week.
   d. **Hydrate.** Continue to make water your drink of choice.
   e. **Eat for Energy.** Continue to add PWR® Foods to your diet and "crowd-out" PWR® Drainers.
   f. **Breathe Deeply.** Continue to practice deep breathing.
   g. **Sleep Soundly.** Continue getting your optimum level and quality of sleep.

4. **CONNECT.** Continue seeking joy. Add at least *20 minutes* playtime every day. Look at your list on page 150.

5. **RELEASE.** Every day, continue to let go of *one* bind – a thought, a thing, a commitment, a relationship, a debt, etc.

Give it your best. Log your Progress.

Week 6 - Progress Log

As you receive PWR® Moves each week, rate yourself daily in each area using a 1 – 5 scale (1 =not successful, 5 =very successful).

Action	Day31	Day32	Day33	Day34	Day35	Day36
REFLECT						
Reflect 20 min.						
FOCUS						
Affirmations						
Program Productivity						
RE-FUEL						
Sweat 30 min.						
Stretch 15 min.						
Strengthen 15 min.						
Hydrate 8 glasses						
Add PWR® Foods						
Breathe Deeply						
Sleep Soundly						
CONNECT						
Seek Joy/Play 20 min.						
RELEASE						
Release 1 Bind						

Accomplishments/Challenges/Notes to Self:

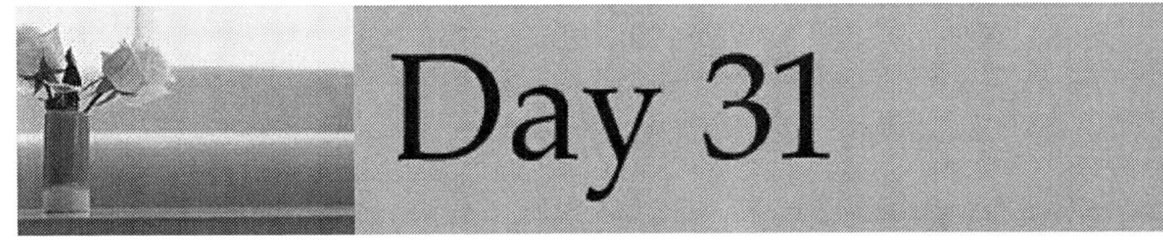

Define the Essentials

"When you know when enough is enough,
there will always be enough."
- Lao-tzu

As you may remember, the fifth principle of Power Living® is **Sanctify your Surroundings**. This is all about detoxifying your environmental energy in order to create an atmosphere that sustains your flow and supports your vision. Ask yourself:

- What are my essentials?
- How can I simplify my life?
- Will more *stuff* make be happy?

Simplicity is about discovering what is *enough* in your life and discarding the rest. Simplicity is not simple. It's a step-by-step process of living with balance. However, once you unburden your Self you will feel a sense of freedom and true prosperity.

The Scarcity Mentality

In our society of over abundance, it's surprising how often our conversations go to how much we *don't* have. From the time we get up in the morning, we're already behind the eight ball! For many of us, we start off thinking: "I didn't get enough sleep." We have already set ourselves up to be inadequate. Then, the media kicks in. The average American sees over 3,000 advertising messages a day. Having taught college consumer marketing and worked in media, I know first-hand the strategies that are employed to make you feel below par. Most ads are created to make you believe you are lacking something and that the only way to be "happy" is to buy their products. This leads to: "I *need* those new boots." "I *need* whiter teeth."

It doesn't end there. These messages reinforce the scarcity mentality. We begin to look for lack... and of course, we find it! It creates a vicious cycle. When you live by the scarcity rule *there is never enough* to go around. It is a manner of thinking which leads to *hoarding* – holding on to things for the fear of loss. You also begin to believe that *more is better* – which leads us to accumulate things. The end result: fear, low self-esteem and a lot of stuff cluttering up your life!

Needs, Wants & Heart Desires

Do you remember the movie *Runaway Bride*? Julia Roberts' character didn't know what type of eggs she liked. She would always order the same kind as her many fiancés. Then, after she left Richard Gere's character at the altar, she took time to really find out what *she* liked. Then, she was finally ready to marry him.

Our process is the same. You must take time to define your essentials. Turn off other peoples' messages and listen to your own inner voice. Determine what will support you on your road to peace and Purpose.

> "Having without possessing... this is supreme virtue."
> - Lao-tzu

Is it a quiet space so you can meditate? Is it an open kitchen so you can cook more often? Go for quality versus quantity. Distinguish between *needs* – food and shelter, *borrowed wants* – a new Lexus, and *heart desires* - a home where you can ride a bike and walk to work. It's okay to want things. The problem occurs when you acquire things mindlessly, and *become defined by and attached to them*. Figure out what you find most satisfying to live simply. Know that if all of the things were taken away tomorrow, you would *still* have enough.

Reality Check

Today we're focused on **simplicity**.

What are my essentials?

What can I release to make space for abundance?

Remember to sweat for at least 30 minutes today.

Day 32

Clear and Cleanse

"I believe that a simple and unassuming manner of life
is best for everyone, best both for the body and the mind."
- Albert Einstein

My Mom always says, "A messy space, a messy mind." There's a lot of truth to that. When there is stuff all around, it's hard to think. Clutter has often been called "visual noise." Ask yourself:

- Am I being drowned out by paper?
- Does my space "sound" dull or agitated?
- Are my closets screaming with old clothes?

Once you define your essentials, get rid of the rest. Seek visual peace and quiet. As you clear away the clutter and cleanse the energy, you will feel a greater sense of clarity.

Clear the Clutter

Here are my "**Top 4 Clutter Critters**:"

1. **Clothes.** If you haven't put it on in the last year get rid of it - unless it's your wedding dress or a special evening suit. If it's torn or worn out, throw it out. If it's in good condition, give it away. I use a 3-to-1 replacement ratio. When you buy three new items, get rid of one old.

2. **Paper.** Handle your paper in one location. Have a wastebasket, shredder and scanner nearby. File or throw away as much as you can. Use technology to consolidate, such as scanning important documents, and using a mobile

PDA/phone for contacts and to-do lists. The IRS offers guidelines on how long certain records must be kept for tax purposes.

3. **Stuff.** This is the "catch-all" category for collectibles and trinkets. Hobbies are nice, but make sure they have a place – preferably tucked away in a cabinet or behind a closed door.

4. **Food.** An overflowing kitchen can sabotage any healthy living plan. Discard leftovers after three days. If you're buying or cooking vegetables or soups in bulk, freeze a portion. Keep the refrigerator organized and the counters clear.

Set a time once a week to clean out an area of your home or office. When it's done in stages, you won't feel overwhelmed and get caught when a deadline hits – such as guests coming.

Cleanse the Energy

Any events accompanied by strong emotions are recorded in the energy around you. If you've ever walked into a room after an argument, you've probably felt the tenseness in the air. Many native cultures believe that this "psychic grunge" accumulates around the edges of room, particularly in corners. This is why many Native Americans, for example, live in round buildings.

There is a specialized branch of Feng Shui from Bali called Space Clearing. This ancient technique can help you clear out the old frequencies and bring in higher levels of energy. Traditionally, you would use Balinese bells. A very simplified version is strong, resonant clapping. Clap in corners to disperse static energy. Imagine unhealthy energy becoming churned up and dispersed, as you create sharp bursts of sound. Then wash your hands in running water. Whether you believe the benefits or not, give it a shot. See if you feel any difference afterwards. If anything, the clapping will energize your physical body and clear your mind!

Reality Check

Today we're focused on **clutter**.

What clutter do I need to remove from my home space?

____

____

____

____

What clutter do I need to remove from my work space?

____

____

____

____

What is my de-clutter strategy? Note exactly when you will commit to clearing and cleansing your spaces.

____

____

____

Remember to practice deep breathing today.

Day 33

Satisfy the Senses

"Light is the first of painters. There is no object
so foul that intense light will not make beautiful."
- Ralph Waldo Emerson

Light, color, scents and sounds all affect us emotionally, physically and spiritually. Ask yourself:

- What sounds calm me down?
- What scents invigorate my mind?
- What colors make me feel happy?

Harmonious home and work spaces simply have good "vibes." When you're feeling right in your space, you are more likely to think clearer, be more productive, and find more peace of mind.

Air & Aroma

Aromatherapy has been used for centuries in many cultures to treat illness and promote well-being. Candles, oils, fresh flowers and herbs can all be used to enhance the atmosphere and change the mood. Only use natural products. Some scents to try are: lavender, clary sage or rosemary for relaxation; peppermint, citrus or eucalyptus for alertness. Clean, pure air also encourages health. Make your space a non-smoking zone. Air rooms daily by opening the windows or using exhaust fans. Check humidity and ventilation. Use natural materials such as scented beeswax for cleaning. By making your space smell more natural, you can improve *all* of your senses!

Light & Color

Light plays a role in regulating the body's biological clock, which controls sleep, hormone production, and other functions. It is also important in treating seasonal affective disorder (SAD), thought to be caused by light deprivation in winter. Let natural light in. Use mirrors to reflect light and bring a feeling of greater space to a room. Avoid lamps with angular designs and direct overhead beams. The low-level electromagnetic fields produced by certain lights, home computers and microwaves may upset metabolism, raise stress and cause allergies – so minimize your exposure.

Color also stimulates our senses, encouraging us to relax or be active. Here are some basic principles melding the Vedic theory of the body's chakras with the Chinese Theory of the Five Elements:

Color Associations		
Color	**Energy**	**Association**
Blue	Harmony, peace, wisdom	Immune system
Purple	Creativity, inspiration, authority	Thyroid glands
Red	Physical energy, vitality, beauty	Heart, Adrenal glands
Orange	Strength, endurance	Sexual organs
Yellow	Mental energy, alertness	Spleen, Stomach
Green	Balance, harmony, prosperity	Thymus gland
White	Purity, health, longevity	Lungs, Large Intestine
Black	Righteousness, spontaneity	Kidney, Bladder

Sounds & Touch

Pleasing sounds encourage relaxation. Think about adding strategically placed wind chimes or the sound of flowing water through a fountain or recorded CD. Classical music is also good for winding down. The use of carpets can reduce unwanted noise, but watch the dust factor. The textures around you can also make you feel sensuous and comfortable. Use natural materials as much as possible, such as pure cotton sheets, lace drapes, and natural woods. Since sweating is so good for the body, you may want to install a sauna in your home – space permitting.

Reality Check

Today we're focused on **the senses**.

How does my home make me feel?

____

____

____

____

What can I add to my home to satisfy my senses?

____

____

____

____

Your Favorites. Test out different scents, colors, textures and sounds. Note the ones that affect you the most positively.

____

____

____

Remember to drink at least 8 glasses of purified water today.

Let the Outside In

"Nature's peace will flow.
into you as sunshine flows into trees."
- John Muir

Since The Power Living® Practice is really about mastering your inner life, this is one of the few times I'll say, "Let the Outside In!" What I'm talking about is Nature. Ask yourself:

- Can I recall the fragrance of fresh rain?
- How much of my food is free of pesticides?
- Do I eat grounding root vegetables in winter and light salads in summer?

Physically and spiritually, we are all connected to the Earth. The cycles of the seasons can affect our disposition and activities. We tend to hibernate in the winter and blossom in the spring. Moods are up with the sun, and subdued with the clouds. Yet, in an environment of increasing stress and desire for speed, it's easy to become disconnected to the world around us. We hop on the subway or in a car. We breathe re-circulated air in an office. It's time to stop and literally smell the roses.

Re-Discover Nature

Nature can have a profound, life-affirming effect on the spirit. It can help us establish inner balance and peace. It can teach us how to live in each moment. It can provide the impetus for spiritual discoveries - inspiring growth and renewal.

Make a point to commune with Nature every day, experiencing her sights, sounds and smells. If it rains, let the water cleanse your spirit. If it is sunny, allow the rays to kiss your skin. Even in a city, it is possible to maintain a connection to the beauty and rhythms of Nature. Though, get away if you must! Here are some ideas:

- Sit on a rock and meditate.
- Allow your feet to touch the ocean.
- Watch the sunset or gaze at the stars.
- Walk in a park or visit a botanical garden.
- Tend a garden – it doesn't even have to be your own!

Other things we've already talked about include: using house plants as a natural purification system and minimizing the use of harmful solvents. Eating in harmony with Nature also helps you connect with the seasons.

Be Environmentally Friendly

Go organic! Food certified under U.S. Dept. of Agriculture regulations as organic must be produced without most synthetic pesticides and fertilizers. Antibiotics, growth hormones, and feed made from animal parts are also banned. Few doubt that high doses of pesticides can cause neurological or reproductive damage – so eating organic is most important for children and pregnant or breast-feeding women, though it can benefit us all.

To lower your food bill and help your local farmers, join a CSA – Community Supported Agriculture. People buy shares in a farm and, in return, enjoy a share of the farm's produce for most of the year. This enables the farmers to thrive and subscribers to get an incredible buy on organic edibles. From June through December, all of my own fruits and vegetables come from a CSA. Go online to find one near you. Also, consider buying environmentally-friendly office and home items. Respect your surroundings and you will receive the rewards of peace and more robust health.

Reality Check

Today we're focused on **Nature**.

What is my favorite experience in Nature?

____

____

How can I live more in harmony with Nature? Make a list of ways you intend to connect with Nature.

1. ______________________________________
2. ______________________________________
3. ______________________________________
4. ______________________________________
5. ______________________________________
6. ______________________________________
7. ______________________________________
8. ______________________________________
9. ______________________________________
10. ______________________________________

Remember to play for at least 20 minutes today.

Day 35

Re-route the Doubters

"No person is your friend who demands your silence,
or denies your right to grow."
- Alice Walker

The people around you also affect your environmental energy. Do you know any psychic vampires? When you're with them it feels like you're in the middle of a horror film. Your energy is just being sucked up minute-to-minute. Ask yourself:

- Are there people around me who drain my energy?
- Do I have a solid Circle of Support?
- Do I exhibit toxic behavior?

Besides being simply annoying and exhausting, being around people with toxic qualities can actually be hazardous to your mental and physical health. If you're not aware of the effect and your own self-esteem is on shaky ground, a barrage of constant negativity can eat away at your Core. The best strategy is to identify the doubters and then re-route the energy.

Practice Verbal Kung-fu

You must protect your energy. First, identify the attackers. You know who they are. They are our blamers and complainers. They usually like to hear their own voices, have a strong need to be right, and love using "the language losers." Some are subtle drainers, starting off as nice and then becoming extremely needy or gossipy. They usually don't take responsibility for their own actions and every conversation is centered on their issues. They tend to escalate problems instead of trying to solve them. Some may verbally cut you off and put you down. Why would you want them around?

The key is to not get pulled into their drama. It's been described as "verbal kung-fu." When you sense a hit is coming, move away. Understand that most toxic people are that way because their own inner lives need work. They may be suffering from low self-esteem or really don't know any better. If you *must* spend time with them, don't engage in negative talk. Always switch to the positive.

"Watch out for false prophets. They come to you in sheep's clothing, but inwardly they are ferocious wolves. By their fruit you will recognize them."
- Matthew 7:15-16

Don't try to change a person. What you can control is your own response. If you know you're in for a stressful encounter, prepare your Self ahead of time with deep breathing and affirmations.

Create your Circle of Support

There is an African Proverb I love: "If a person dreams alone, it remains nothing but a dream. But when a people dream together, that dream can become a reality." Having supporters and a few good friends are crucial to your success. This is your Circle of Support. Look for people who understand your life vision and will bring out the best in you. A true supporter believes in you when you don't believe in your Self; listens without judging; shares joy in your success; prays for you when you're in pain; encourages your dreams; and offers constructive advice. Honor their intentions, welcome their encouragement, and show gratitude for their existence. And as Matthew 7:13 says, "Enter through the narrow gate." In other words, keep the circle tight with just those few people who will be your coaches, cheerleaders and reality checks. Keep the doubters out!

Reality Check

Today we're focused on **toxic people**.

Who in my current circle drains my energy?

____

____

____

____

How will I protect my energy from them?

____

____

____

____

Who is in my Circle of Support?

____

____

____

____

Remember to stretch for at least 15 minutes today.

Day 36

Seek Financial Serenity

"Empty pockets never held anyone back.
Only empty heads and empty hearts can do that."
- Norman Vincent Peale

You may be thinking, "I would love to live in a quiet space close to Nature and walk to work, but how can I afford it?" Since I have a Harvard MBA and worked in a finance capacity for many years, I would be remiss if we didn't talk about money. Ask yourself:

- Am I valuing my time effectively?
- What role does order play in my financial life?
- Does my prosperity plan reflect my life vision?

Again, it's about self-awareness and self-control. What is your current relationship with money? How do you treat it and how does it respond to you? My Mom always says you have to *respect your money*. What she means is honor the penny as well as the dollar. Many of us ignore the change. If we drop a dime, we leave it there on the ground because it's metal not paper. That dime, over time, can finance your dream.

Plan for Prosperity

Strive for financial serenity as well as security. Go back to your essentials. Ask yourself: "What will bring me peace and support my Purpose? What does *prosperity* mean to me?" Prosperity is so much more than money. It represents freedom. It's about making choices so you can experience joy, right now *and* over the long-term – not just fleeting happiness. Instead of hiring a financial planner who will push products, find a partner who will respect your vision and offer relevant advice that will get you there.

Whether you are a corporate executive, a stay-at-home mom or a retiree, you are the Director and CEO of your life. Here are my "**Four Financial Operating Principles:**"

1. **Order your financial life.** Keep your records straight. Know where everything is in your financial world. My mantra is: "Eyes Wide Open." Know where your money is going so you can re-direct it if you need to – that's empowerment!

2. **Value your time and money.** Respect the dimes as well as the dollars. Think before you buy, and save while you pay down debt. If you can make more money during the time you would normally do a chore, hire it out.

3. **Make money while you sleep.** We are all entrepreneurs of sorts. Even if you have a 9-to-5 job, think of passive income. Your goal is to have the time to pursue your passions. Think of something you can invest time in *once* that then continues to pay you, like real estate or creative royalty income.

4. **Honor the flow.** Circulate your money. Take pleasure in the experiences it can provide for you and then release it. Give at least 10% to things you care about – your faith, family, etc.

You don't have to be rich, to live richly. It goes back to choice. William A. Ward reflects on this topic nicely: "Before you speak, listen. Before you write, think. Before you spend, earn. Before you invest, investigate. Before you criticize, wait. Before you pray, forgive. Before you quit, try. Before you retire, save. Before you die, give." One very important thing to remember: If you have taken the time to discover your Purpose – that one thing you are suited for better than anyone else, *and* you commit to releasing it in the world, you *will* create financial abundance and live a truly prosperous life.

Reality Check

Today we're focused on **prosperity**.

What do I need to do to bring more order to my financial life?

How can I make money while I sleep?

How can I honor the flow?

Remember to eat some PWR® Foods today.

A PWR® Moment

My New Old Friend

The Power of Letting Go

I used to hang on to just about everything – worn-out clothes, old papers, even my previous job identity. I was following the "just in case" philosophy. "I'll keep this just in case I have an occasion to wear a big taffeta dress… just in case I need research on the online industry from 10 years ago… just in case they don't take me seriously as an entrepreneur."

I was even hanging on to an old beau. I would run through my mind decisions we had made at certain points in our courtship. "If I had said yes, we would be together now. If we had just talked about it, he would have understood." That inner dialogue was consuming my energy for years. To top it off, every man I met would have to live up to the vision of my bygone love. Since the perfect union was really an illusion, nobody measured up. When I finally forgave him for prior transgressions, took charge of my own choices, and spent time developing my spiritual life, I was able to let go and let in more fulfilling relationships.

Now that he's married and I'm happily involved, we have been able to get back to a deep soul connection - the thing that attracted us to each other in the first place. We both have said goodbye to hurts from the past, and have welcomed in a new relationship based on the Present. He has become my new old friend!

Week 7:

Integrate the Principles

Week 7 – PWR® Moves

Welcome to our final week! Congratulations! You've now gotten all the primary habits started. This week, we've going to maintain them, as well as plan for the future.

1. **REFLECT.** Continue to reflect for at least *20 minutes a day* – 10 minutes in the morning, 10 minutes in the evening.

2. **FOCUS.** Continue tuning your mind with positive affirmations every day, at least three times a day. Continue to program your productivity for peak performance.

3. **RE-FUEL.** Continue the basics:

    a. **Sweat.** Continue cardiovascular for at least *30 minutes a day*, for the 6 days of our week.
    b. **Stretch.** Continue stretching for at least *15 minutes a day*, for the 6 days of our week.
    c. **Strengthen.** Continue strengthening for at least *15 minutes a day*, for the 6 days of our week.
    d. **Hydrate.** Continue to make water your drink of choice.
    e. **Eat for Energy.** Continue to add PWR® Foods to your diet and "crowd-out" PWR® Drainers.
    f. **Breathe Deeply.** Continue to practice deep breathing.
    g. **Sleep Soundly.** Continue getting your optimum level and quality of sleep.

4. **CONNECT.** Continue seeking joy, including at least *20 minutes* of playtime every day.

5. **RELEASE.** Every day, continue to let go of *one* bind – a thought, a thing, a commitment, a relationship, a debt, etc.

Give it your best. Log your Progress.

Week 7 - Progress Log

As you receive PWR® Moves each week, rate yourself daily in each area using a 1 – 5 scale (1 =not successful, 5 =very successful).

Action	Day37	Day38	Day39	Day40 and Beyond...		
REFLECT						
Reflect 20 min.						
FOCUS						
Affirmations						
Program Productivity						
RE-FUEL						
Sweat 30 min.						
Stretch 15 min.						
Strengthen 15 min.						
Hydrate 8 glasses						
Add PWR® Foods						
Breathe Deeply						
Sleep Soundly						
CONNECT						
Seek Joy/Play 20 min.						
RELEASE						
Release 1 Bind						

Accomplishments/Challenges/Notes to Self:

Re-Assess the Situation

"The life which is unexamined is not worth living."
- Plato

How do you feel? Have you learned anything? Have you taken positive action? Over the next four days we're going to re-assess, plan for the future and, of course, claim your victory! Right now let's review the Five Principles of Power Living®:

1. **Live on Purpose** – You assessed your gifts, defined your core values and beliefs, and aligned your spiritual energy to be more Present and on Purpose.
2. **Tune your Mind to the Positive** – You checked your thoughts and language, and learned how to focus your mental energy to create positive manifestations and spur inspiration.
3. **Honor your Body** – You learned PWR® Foods and "The 7 Rules of PWR® Eating," as well as how to exercise, breathe and sleep to maximize your physical energy for peak performance and optimum health.
4. **Be a Humble Warrior** – You practiced leading with your heart, and learned how to engage your emotional energy to cultivate an attitude of gratitude and build intimate connections, steady joy and strong faith in your path.
5. **Sanctify your Surroundings** – You learned how to detoxify your environmental energy to sustain your flow and create support and simplicity in your home, relationships and finances.

Let's see how you've evolved…

Reality Check

After thirty-six full days of introspection, let's do another overall check of where you are now. From your new perspective, answer the following:

Who Am I?

Who am I at my Core? Who am I becoming? Describe your Authentic Self. Who are you at your best? Remember to strip away the labels and get down to the Core.

Remember to sweat, stretch & strengthen every day.

Core values. Can you list them off the top of your head? Have they changed over the last couple of weeks?

1. ____

2. ____

3. ____

4. ____

5. ____

What is my vision? What is your Personal Vision Statement now? Has it changed?

What is my passion? What would you do with your life if you had no limits of time or money? Has it become clearer?

Where Am I?

Where am I along my path? How big is the gap between where you are now and who you are meant to be? Has it changed? Take a moment to think about where you are right now:

- **Spiritual**: Do I take time to cultivate my inner life? Am I living my core values? Do I operate by faith or by fear?
- **Mental**: Do my thoughts support my vision? Am I focused, engaged and productive at work?
- **Physical**: Am I honoring my body by how I breathe, eat, drink, sleep, and exercise?
- **Emotional**: Am I able to make deep connections? Do I experience joy every day? Do I have the patience to succeed?
- **Environmental**: Does my environment - space, people, things - support my life vision? Are my finances reflecting a flow in my life or blockage?

5					
4					
3					
2					
1					
	Spiritual	**Mental**	**Physical**	**Emotional**	**Environmental**

Remember to decide what number represents your current state in each category: 1 = disappointing, 5 = ideal. Then, for each category, mark a large dot on the line corresponding to that number. Connect the dots to see if your energy is being optimally utilized or if it is off-balance. If you "flat-line" on 1 across the board, then we need to revive you! If your chart looks like a roller-coaster, then you need to balance it out by working on the low areas. If your numbers are high and level, then you are Power Living® and can focus on maintaining your positive habits.

Review your Numbers

Weight: ______ Height: _______ BMI: _______

Body mass index (BMI) is a measure of body fat based on height and weight that applies to both adult men and women. Find your number below:

Body Mass Index

Weight in Pounds

Height in Feet and Inches	120	130	140	150	160	170	180	190	200	210	220	230	240	250
4'6	29	31	34	36	39	41	43	46	48	51	53	56	58	60
4'8	27	29	31	34	36	38	40	43	45	47	49	52	54	56
4'10	25	27	29	31	34	36	38	40	42	44	46	48	50	52
5'0	23	25	27	29	31	33	35	37	39	41	43	45	47	49
5'2	22	24	26	27	29	31	33	35	37	38	40	42	44	46
5'4	21	22	24	26	28	29	31	33	35	37	38	40	41	43
5'6	19	21	23	24	26	28	29	31	33	34	36	37	39	40
5'8	18	20	21	23	24	26	27	29	31	32	34	35	37	38
5'10	17	19	20	22	23	24	26	27	29	30	32	33	35	36
6'0	16	18	19	20	22	23	24	26	27	29	30	31	33	34
6'2	15	17	18	19	21	22	23	24	26	27	28	30	31	32
6'4	15	16	17	18	20	21	22	23	24	26	27	28	29	30
6'6	14	15	16	17	19	20	21	22	23	24	25	27	28	29
6'8	13	14	15	17	18	19	20	21	22	23	24	25	26	28

☐ Underweight ■ Healthy Weight ☐ Overweight ■ Obese

	Your Number:	Normal/Good Range:
Blood Pressure:	__________	*120/80 mmHg*
Blood Glucose:	__________	*4 to 8mmol/l*
Total Cholesterol:	__________	*Less than 200 mg/dL*
HDL: ("good" cholesterol)	__________	*60 mg/dL or above*
LDL: ("bad" cholesterol)	__________	*100-129 mg/dL*
Waist Measurement:	__________	*Women >35in. Men >40in.*

Notes: 1) Blood glucose is higher after meals and usually lowest in the morning. 2) To measure your waist, place a tape measure around your bare abdomen just above your hip bone. Be sure that the tape is snug, but does not compress your skin, and is parallel to the floor. 3) BMI does not show the difference between fat and muscle, so it does not always accurately predict when weight could lead to health problems – particularly for people who are very short (under 5 feet) or have a lot of muscle.

Day 38

Plan for Success

"A good plan today is better
than a perfect plan tomorrow."
- George S. Patton

The Bible says, "A man reaps what he sows." In other words, success is a planned outcome not an accident. It comes from *deciding* what you want to accomplish and *focusing your energy* on only those things that will move you toward that goal. Now that you've re-assessed where you are, ask yourself:

- Where am I now compared to Day 1?
- Is my outlook different?
- How do I want to continue what I've learned?

Now, it's time to plan for the future. A plan is like a map. It helps you know where you're going, what you will need along the way, how far you are from your destination, and which route will best get you there. The process of planning forces you to crystallize your vision. It brings the future into the Present through your daily activities, and allows you to foresee potential problems.

First, write down your goals to give them concrete form. The key is to be specific. It is not good enough to say that you want to "be rich" or "lose weight." Each goal should be measurable, with a realistic deadline attached to it. Next, break down the major goals into simple, ordered tasks. Finally, take the first step. A plan is no good unless you act upon it.

Reality Check

What Must I Do To Be Me?

What *must* I do every day to be authentically me? Look at the results of your energy utilization. Where are you now in relation to where you want to be? Again, be honest. It's for your eyes only.

What do I need to add to my life?

1. ______

2. ______

3. ______

4. ______

5. ______

What do I need to remove?

1. ______

2. ______

3. ______

4. ______

5. ______

Make sure your goals are SMART –
Specific, Measurable, Attainable, Realistic, and Time-specific.

What <u>three goals</u> would I like to accomplish within the next <u>three months</u>?

How would it feel to have those three goals accomplished?

What <u>one major goal</u> would I like to accomplish within the next <u>twelve months</u>?

How would accomplishing that major goal affect my life?

Remember to pause and play every day.

What is my long-term goal (4-5 years)?

What smaller goals will get me there?

How can I start right now?

What 5 things do I want to *experience* in my lifetime?

1.

2.

3.

4.

5.

Day 39

Take Consistent Action

"Vision without action is merely a dream.
Action without vision just passes the time.
Vision with action can change the world."
-- Joel Barker

There have been many people with no skills and a poor plan who have succeeded because they stuck with it. They managed to hold on long after others had given up.

Perseverance -- steady persistence in adhering to a course of action, a belief, or Purpose -- is one of the most important keys to success. It can build character, make up for deficiencies in talent, and lead you to triumph.

> "Big shots are only little shots who keep shooting."
> - Christopher Morley

As Solomon explained in the Bible: "The race is not to the swift... or wealth to the brilliant." As long as you are determined and move forward, no matter how slow, you *will* get to your destination. Be Present at every step along the way. There is a reason and a season for everything. Persevering in difficult times tests your faith and commitment, and forces you to be creative. It prepares you to *receive* your Highest Good.

Procrastination comes from fear, or lack of direction. Action is the food that will nourish your success. Even a small step will move you closer to your destination, and increase your confidence. Once you start, unforeseen circumstances will help propel you forward. If you make a mistake, you will learn and grow in the process.

Set out today to cultivate and share your unique gifts with the world. Think of each inspired thought as a gift from God. Honor it with immediate action. Otherwise, the urgency will diminish and you will lose the initial enthusiasm and throw away the Present. Begin where you are, with whatever you have. Be mindful and specific in your actions. Using your Core as the guide, follow the **Power Living® A.C.T.I.O.N. Process**:

- **A**rticulate your Goal
- **C**heck your Values
- **T**ighten the Parameters
- **I**nitiate Action
- **O**wn the Process
- **N**ote your Progress

When asked to describe significant regrets in their lives, most people focus on actions they did *not* take rather than actions they did. Tomorrow is not promised.

> "We cannot cross the sea merely by staring at the water."
> - Raindranath Tagore

However, don't be afraid of death; be afraid of never living. Live each day purposely with joy and passion. Life will pass you by if you wait until conditions are "perfect" in order to realize your divine destiny. Start participating in life. Things will not always go as you plan, but know that the Divine Plan for you is good. Learn from the detours, and keep taking steps toward your vision. Planning purposefully and acting persistently is a sure path to progress. If you feel like you're about to quit hold on a bit longer. The brightest light often comes right after the darkest night. Realize that the only true failure is *not* trying to pursue what is in your heart. As the Nike commercial says, "Just Do It!"

My PWR® Foods

What foods make me feel good? Now that you've hopefully experimented with some PWR® Foods, make a list of items that really make *you* feel good - not the fake high of processed sugar - real sustaining energy!

1. ____________________

2. ____________________

3. ____________________

4. ____________________

5. ____________________

6. ____________________

7. ____________________

8. ____________________

9. ____________________

10. ____________________

11. ____________________

12. ____________________

Remember to "crowd-out" the PWR® Drainers every day.

Claim your Freedom

"...people are as free as they want to be."
- James Baldwin

Congratulations for reaching Day 40! You've now learned the foundation principles and practices of Power Living®. You are on your way to becoming a New World PWR® Broker. Claim your freedom. Ask yourself:

- What does it mean to be free?
- Is my freedom really dependent on someone else?
- Is it a state of mind?

I think by now you know the answer. America offers considerable liberties to its citizens relative to other nations. We expect such democratic ideals as "freedom of speech," and "freedom of worship." However, our very culture -- driven by values of material comfort and external conformity -- can also enslave us.

We tend to be followers; slaves to our jobs, our lifestyles, family expectations, and media images. As Dr. W.E.B. DuBois said, "Freedom is a state of mind." A person can be free even within prison walls. Bondage or liberation is in your own mind.

"Destiny is not matter of chance. It is a matter of choice. It is not a thing to be waited for it is a thing to be achieved."
- William Jennings Bryan

Think about why children smile so often. They live in the Present moment and are not afraid to express how they feel. They haven't yet been shackled by judgment and beliefs.

The American Heritage dictionary defines freedom as: "the capacity to exercise choice." **Your everyday success is dependent upon making good choices, and aligning those choices with your personal vision.** Choose wisely. Start living your own truth. If you want to be healthy, choose whole foods. If you want positive relationships, choose to be loving. Start small, and remember that non-action is also a choice that may have long-lasting results.

- Choose love… instead of hate.
- Choose faith… instead of fear.
- Choose health… instead of disease.
- Choose praise… instead of gossip.
- Choose empathy… instead of judgment.
- Choose action… instead of procrastination.
- Choose life… instead of a living death.

Make a declaration of war against negativity. Unlock the chains of fear and compliance, and allow the authentic YOU to emerge. *Only then,* will you truly be free. Your commitment doesn't end on Day 40. This is just the beginning of Power Living®.

Share your Secrets

Remember the elements of our New World: "Power is not defined by how much control you have over *others,* but how much control you have over your *Self.* It's not about how many things you *acquire.* It's about how many people you *inspire."*

> "Do not go where the path may lead, go instead where there is no path and leave a trail."
> - Emerson

Who is waiting to benefit from your gifts? Why keep them waiting? As 1 Timothy 5:15-16 says, "Do not neglect your gift… Be diligent in these matters; give yourself wholly to them, so that everyone may see your progress. Watch your life and doctrine closely. Persevere in them, because if you do, you will save both yourself and your hearers."

Reality Check

The ultimate goal of 40 Days to Power Living® was for you to get in the habit of *consciousness* and *action*, allowing you to realize true **PWR® - Purpose With Results™**. How did you do? Take a moment to reflect on your accomplishments.

What did I accomplish over the 40 Days to Power Living®?

____

____

____

____

____

____

How does the outcome make me feel?

____

____

____

____

____

Who am I going to inspire? How?

<u>**Commitment Statement**</u>**.** Write a pledge to your Self outlining your commitment to living a purposeful life going forward.

Remember to share your PWR® – Purpose With Results™ every day.

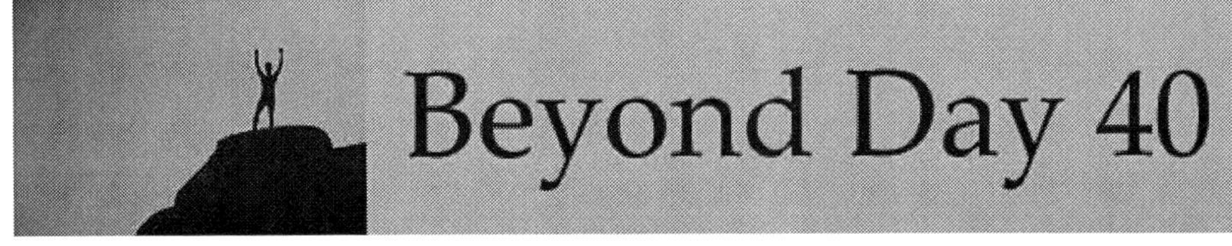

Experiment & Experience

"Use your gifts faithfully, and they shall be enlarged;
practice what you know, and you shall attain to higher knowledge."
- Matthew Arnold

Now what? On Day 41 are you truly Power Living®? Only you can know! I've given you the framework to close the gap between where you are now and who you are becoming. Ask yourself:

- Am I more aware of my habits?
- Can I now identify my own blocks?
- Has my perspective changed in any area of my life?
- Have I learned at least *one* concept I can use that will positively affect my growth?

If you answered "Yes" to any of these questions – even if you did not complete every Reality Check in the book - then you have been successful. You have moved toward *consciousness* and, hopefully, *action*. I followed the concept of specificity by titling this book "40 Days *to* Power Living®" instead of "40 Days *of* Power Living®". Remember, I generally work with clients over at least a three-month period. I knew that it would take you *at least* 40 days to receive the basic principles. Now the real work begins!

As my Mom has said: "This is the Beginning of Knowing… the beginning of all there is to be. You will become that which you have decided to become." So, now that you know, what will you do? It's up to you. Are you content to simply survive or are you committed to thrive? It's your choice. Set your intention; make a decision, and then act!

Practice Living

The Power Living® Practice is called such because it's not a one-time deal. You have to *practice and live it every day*. It's not an intellectual exercise. It's experiential – which means these principles need to become ingrained in your subconscious and manifest in your behavior.

Experiment and experience - the same process you used when selecting your PWR® Foods. For example, if finding 15 minutes of reflection time in the morning has been challenging, then commit to five minutes instead if that will make it more consistent. Find out what works for you and then do it. Practice it and live it!

> "We learn by practice. Whether it means to learn to dance by practicing dancing or to learn to live by practicing living, the principles are the same. One becomes in some area an athlete of God."
> - Martha Graham

If you get off-track one day, then self-correct the next day. Don't get discouraged. Remind your Self that *this is a Practice*. Use the review time in the evening to ask, "How did I do today? What do I intend to do differently tomorrow?" That ritual helps you close the gap between who you are and who you are becoming. It all goes back to the Three Core Questions, "Who Am I?, Where Am I? and What *Must* I Do To Be Me?" Keep asking those questions.

You don't have to do it alone. Tap into your Circle of Support. Recruit a commitment partner. Create a study group. Now that you are conscious, you have a greater responsibility for your wellbeing and success. You can not plead ignorance. Commit to Life. Be an active investigator of your Self. From this day forward, understand that *everything* you do is a choice. You do not "have to" do anything. Be fully Present living as if *this* is the last day to enjoy your Gift. Start Power Living® today!

The Power Living® Practice

Now that you understand The Power Living® Practice, the key is to make it a *daily* ritual. Remember the Primary Habits and 5 Trigger Words below:

1 REFLECT Live on Purpose Quiet time in morning to reflect Quiet time in evening to review	**2 FOCUS** Tune your Mind to the Positive Affirmations, Breath Prayers Prime Work - Peak Energy Time Break every 90-120 minutes News Fast once a week
3 RE-FUEL Honor your Body Sweat for 30 minutes a day; Stretch for 15; Strengthen for 15 Drink 8 glasses of water a day Breathe Deeply; Sleep Soundly Eat for Energy every 3 hours Fast once a week	**The Power Living® Practice**
4 CONNECT Be a Humble Warrior Play & Laugh at least 20 minutes every day. Love your Self & others	**5 RELEASE** Sanctify your Surroundings Let go of one bind - a thing, a thought, a task, a commitment, person, debt, every day

A PWR® Moment

The Dividing Line

The Power of Personal Responsibility

Two days after holding the first printed "galley" proof of this book in my hands, I was scheduled to begin a *40 Days to Power Living®* program at the nationally renowned Abyssinian Baptist Church in New York City. The pastor's wife, Mrs. Patricia Butts, was leading the health ministry. I was honored to be graced by her support and excited to see how this material would be used.

A day before the Lenten event, I received a call from one of the parishioners. Reverend Butts had announced the program at the previous sermon, so we were expecting a full house for the kick-off. The woman on the phone said she wanted more information, but it seemed like she had one very specific question on her mind. She asked, "Am I going to have to *do* anything?" It took me a moment to really hear her meaning. The question was similar to the mentality I've seen in many people with energy that has become depleted. They are searching for a "quick-fix" solution.

Thankfully, when I led the first workshop, the crowd was much more open to transformation. There were men and women of all ages who went through the 40-day program together. Some people lost weight; some tamed their inner critic; others focused on distancing toxic people. They did the work and realized change. The experience reinforced something I already knew: there is a dividing line between those who *want* to take control of their lives and those who are spiritually asleep. Once you step over the line and take responsibility for your destiny, you are well on your way to Power Living®!

"And this is my prayer:
that your love may abound more and more
in knowledge and depth of insight,
so that you may be able to discern what is best..."

- Philippians 1:9-10

About the Author

Teresa Kay-Aba Kennedy is President of Power Living Enterprises, Inc., which offers transformational programs and products, and Founder of Ta Yoga, operating one of the first yoga studios in Harlem – the Ta Yoga House. Before becoming a wellness activist and entrepreneur, she was Vice President of Business Operations at MTV Networks – where she negotiated landmark media deals bringing in over $30 million, founding and running one of the few profitable digital media businesses at the time. She also consulted and wrote case studies on *Fortune 500* companies for Harvard Business School, and worked as a Creative Consultant for Universal Studios.

Although her parents are American, Terri was born in Ghana, schooled in Australia and Italy. She has a dual B.A. in Sociology & Design from Wellesley College, and an MBA from Harvard Business School. She is certified as a Holistic Health Counselor, Yoga Instructor, Group Fitness Instructor, Personal Trainer, and Lifestyle & Weight Management Counselor. She is on the faculty of the Institute of Integrative Nutrition, and is currently working on a Ph.D. in World Religions.

Terri is a sought-after motivational speaker working with entities ranging from Eileen Fisher and *W Magazine* to the Social Venture Network and the *Black Enterprise* Entrepreneurs Conference. She has been featured in media ranging from CNN, FOX, NBC's *Today in New York, The Hallmark Channel,* and *ARD TV* in Germany to *The New York Times, Prevention, Yoga Journal, Essence* and Oprah's book *Live Your Best Life*! She is author of three case studies published under Harvard Business School Publishing, and producer of a variety of Power Living® products. She is on the Board of Directors of Yoga Alliance, and is a 2006-2007 participant in the Emerging Entrepreneurs Program: An *Inc.* magazine - William J. Clinton Foundation Partnership. She has received a number of awards, including *The Network Journal's 40 Under Forty Achievement Award.*

Power Living® Programs

Power Living Enterprises, Inc. is dedicated to helping people from *all* walks of life, live better lives. Programs include executive and life coaching - in-person, via telephone and email, group workshops, Ta Yoga™ sessions, personal & professional development programs for corporations and associations, and motivational speaking. Power Living® products include:

40 DAYS TO POWER LIVING®

Think, Eat & Live on Purpose

This inspirational how-to guide gives you the framework to craft your divinely appointed life... *from the inside out.* It includes day-to-day goals for you to charge your spiritual, mental, physical, emotional and environmental energy. You can sign up online for an interactive component where you will receive additional affirmations, recipes, and much more!

THE POWER LIVING® PLEDGE

An Affirmation for a Purposeful & Powerful Life

This small book can help you stay on track with The Power Living® Practice. It encapsulates all of the principles of Power Living® into *one* affirmation that can be repeated every day as a reminder of how to live. It also acts as a PWR® Book – designed to include your personal mission, core values, favorite quotes, PWR® Foods and other essentials.

POWER LIVING®: MINI-ESCAPES CD

Relaxation Techniques for Any Situation

This guided relaxation program will calm the body and mind, allowing you to take *a vacation from your busy life.* From breath awareness and visualization to meditation and affirmations, it offers 70 minutes of 3-to-12-minute instant relaxation breaks.

SEVEN-DAY PWR® DETOX

Cleanse your Body, Mind & Spirit

This seven-day guided detoxification program focuses on *nutritious juices and whole foods* you can find in your local store. There are no expensive detoxification formulas to buy. The core elements of the program include a specialized meal plan, hydrotherapy, self-care strategies, specific breathing techniques and yoga poses. Full program includes the book, an audio seminar, an online video and email coaching.

PWR® BRANDED APPAREL & ACCESSORIES

Make a statement with your life by wearing PWR® branded apparel and accessories. Let others know that you are actively seeking true PWR® - Purpose With Results™! A percent of the proceeds go to build our "Young PWR® Brokers Program," which teaches positive life skills to youth ages 5 to 25. Our vision is to create a world of confident, creative, caring and conscious young leaders who are achieving through authenticity and inspiring others to do the same.

THE GIFT OF EMPOWERMENT

Give the gift of empowerment. Donate selected Power Living® products to one of the incredible non-profits in our chosen list of PWR® Affiliates. Whether it is one item or 10,000, your sponsored gift will help us spread the message of wellness to worthy programs supporting youth groups and underserved communities. Receive a tax-deduction for your gift, as well as recognition as a PWR® Broker. Go online to www.power-living.com for more information.

Become a New World PWR® Broker

Sign up for our free monthly newsletter.
Visit us online at **www.power-living.com** or call **212-289-6363.**
To learn more about Ta Yoga™, go to **www.tayoga.com.**